SAILING
TO WIN

I0081228

GLOBAL
PUBLISHING
GROUP

Global Publishing Group
Australia • New Zealand • Singapore • America • London

SAILING TO WIN

Guaranteed Winning Strategies To Navigate From The Back To The Front Of The Fleet

DINGHIES AND ONE DESIGN

Brett Bowden

First Edition 2017

National Library of Australia

Cataloguing-in-Publication entry:

Creator: Bowden, Brett Antony, author.

Title: Sailing to Win: Guaranteed Winning Strategies to Navigate From the Back to the Front of the Fleet / Brett Antony Bowden.

ISBN: 9781925288360 (paperback)

Subjects: Sailboats
Sailboat racing – Rules
Sailboat racing – Psychological aspects.

Published by Global Publishing Group
PO Box 517 Mt Evelyn, Victoria 3796 Australia
Email info@GlobalPublishingGroup.com.au

For further information about orders:
Phone: +61 3 9739 4686 or Fax +61 3 8648 6871

I dedicate this book to all the sailors who turn up every week, compete their hearts out but always go home with the boiled lollies. It is those sailors who want to improve that this book was written for.

Brett Bowden

ACKNOWLEDGEMENTS

It has been a privilege to write this book.

As with any major project, there are a number of very special people who contributed to making this book happen, so I'd like to take this opportunity to say "THANK YOU".

Firstly, I'd like to thank my Mentor Darren Stephens who was the inspiration for this book, I needed someone to tell me I could do it.

A special Thank You to the contributing Olympians, national champions and sailing legends featured in this book. Your willingness to share your tips and secrets with competing sailors who want to challenge you on the water, is a priceless gift. It has been a tremendous privilege to work with every one of you and I'm sure that thousands of sailors will be influenced positively by the insights and knowledge that you've shared.

To my friends who promised not to laugh when I said I was going to write a book on how to improve your competitive sailing. Thanks for your words of encouragement, there are too many to list here but your best wishes made it an even more enjoyable task.

A big thank you to Kelly and the team from Darren's office for their willingness to attend to the ongoing changes and technological challenges that I have put them through. Thanks for your guidance, patience and flexibility!

And finally, a huge Thank You to our publisher, Global Publishing Group for your dedication and commitment to the book's success.

FREE BONUS GIFT
Valued at $297 – But Yours **FREE!**

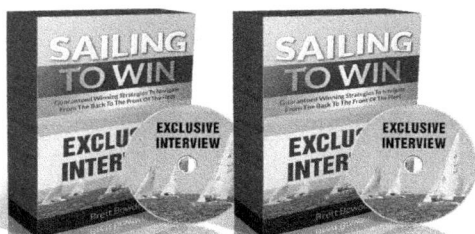

Claim your **FREE BONUS GIFTS** by going to
www.SailingToWin.com/FreeGift

Look! Make sure you grab your FREE Key Tips and Secrets from Two High Achievers in sailing.

- **BONUS #1:** Excerpts from RARE and Exclusive interviews with Roger Blasse, OK dinghy, twice world champion and 14-foot skiff sailing legend.

- **BONUS #2:** Excerpts from an exclusive interview with Mat Bugg, silver medallist in the 2.4 metre class at the recent Rio Paralympics.

Roger and Mat share their preparation procedures, racing secrets, tips and strategies to help you improve your regatta results in these exclusive video programs.

Claim your **FREE BONUS GIFTS NOW** by going to
www.SailingToWin.com/FreeGift

CONTENTS

FOREWORD

John Bertrand, AO

As the skipper of Australia II, winning the America's Cup was definitely one of my career highlights.

Even 25 years on I'm still amazed by the people who stop to tell me what they were doing when they watched my team cross the finishing line in Newport, USA.

As a champion sailor it's always one of your goals to try and win the race!

If you want to be at the front of the fleet, preparation, knowledge and time on the water play an increasing role in dictating where you end up on the leader board.

The level of ability that ensured success a year ago will no longer guarantee the same result today. If you are no longer striving to improve you can be sure that someone else in your fleet will be.

Yacht racing is one of the most highly complex and competitive sports, and not only requires a high degree of skill, but to succeed you must possess the attributes of judgement, teamwork, concentration, split-second decision making and above all patience.

What makes yacht racing stand out is that unlike many other sporting pursuits, to be successful you must deal with many factors outside your control such as wind, tide or current, state of the sea, ever-changing weather conditions and your mindset – no two races or events are ever the same.

International author and sailor Brett Bowden has masterfully tied together all the aspects necessary to concentrate on in order to steadily improve. It is by no means the whole story but contains the building blocks to start your journey up the leader board.

In putting this book together, the author has used his own experiences and has also learned from interviews with high achieving sailors from many different classes and from different countries in order to help those of us who want to improve.

The sailors that have contributed to this book are happy for fellow competitors to get faster and to push them, because being challenged is how they get better as well.

John Bertrand

John Bertrand, AO

John Bertrand with Alan Bond holding the Americas Cup trophy in 1983.

INTRODUCTION

The purpose of this book is to help experienced competitive sailors like me who have sailed regularly, some of us for many years, but have enjoyed little success.

Perhaps we have seen our results plateau or, heaven forbid, even seen a steady decline in our regatta placings.

Some of the information contained in this book may already be known and practised by you, so skip past that and concentrate on learning the things that will give you the improvement you desire.

I believe that by learning, getting help and advice from legends and high achievers from our sport and acting on the tips that they give us in this book, we will improve the average finishing position at competitions, whether it be club, national or international regattas.

To achieve this improvement, we need to work on our weaknesses and the best results will come from working on what we are bad at.

It's fun to practise in conditions that we enjoy the most but we need to get outside our comfort zone and practise in those conditions we are not good at, to finally enjoy better results.

The aim of this book is to get you closer to the front of the fleet and who knows, you may even get to mix it with Olympians and world champions, if that is your aim.

THE PEOPLE I INTERVIEWED

Andrew "Doggy" Palfrey

Country:	UK (Born in Australia)
Club:	RPAYC (AUS) RBYC (AUS)
When you started sailing:	Aged 9
Class started sailing in?	12-foot cadet
Classes you have sailed?	Star, Etchells, Farr 40, J24, Soling, 12- foot cadet.
Currently sailing:	Star

Sailing Achievements:

Multiple World Champion as an athlete and coach in highly competitive America's Cup, Olympic and international class levels.

From beginning working in chandleries, as a sailing instructor, running events and building boats, Andrew has progressed to becoming a professional athlete and coach at the highest levels of the sport in Olympics, America's Cup and other international competitions.

Olympics

- Olympian represented Australia at Beijing Games, Star class with Iain Murray, 2008
- 8th place Star World's, sailing with Iain Murray, 2008
- 9th place Star World's, sailing with Iain Murray, 2007
- Qualified Australia for Olympic Games, 2008
- Competed in all Sailing World Cup events, Star class, 2006 & 2007

Coaching

- Head Coach and training camp management – America's Cup challenger of record, Artemis racing, 2010–2013
- Coach 18ft-skiff multiple World Champion, "Gotta Love It 7" Steve Jarmin, 2006–2009
- Coach BMW Oracle Racing USA Team Louis Vuitton Trophy, Nice, 2009
- Coach Farr40 Australian Champion, Transfusion, 2009

Event Management

- Regatta Director – Airlie Beach Race Week 2003–2004
- Event Organiser – Etchells Worlds, Melbourne Australia, 1995

Plus

- 2009 – 3rd Etchells Worlds, Melbourne Australia.
- 2010 – 1st 5.5 Metre Worlds, Lake Garda Italy.
- 2010 – 1st Etchells Worlds, Dublin Ireland.

Dr Gavin Dagley

Consulting psychologist, executive coach with a reputation for results and performance development.

Country:	Australia/New Zealand
Club:	Port Melbourne Yacht Club
When you started sailing:	Aged 12
Class started sailing in?	Idle Along
Classes you have sailed?	Laser, Flying Dutchman, 470, Flying 15, Etchells, 14-foot skiff, sailboard, OK dinghy
Currently sailing:	Laser

Sailing Achievements:

- 2016 1st Laser World Grand Masters, Nuevo, Mexico
- 21 national title podium finishes
- 5 World and International regatta top-10 finishes
- 21 podium finishes at National Championships, and 5 top-10 finishes in the 8 World and International regattas he has completed, including 2 wins.

Gavin has received Yachting Victoria awards for "Contribution to Yachting" and "Coaching Program of the Year."

He is a published sailing writer on the technical aspects of yacht racing with more than 10 years of regular contributions to US-based magazine *Sailing World*.

As a designer, his sailboard and 14-foot skiff designs have both won their respective National Championships.

Gavin has also completed more than 10,000 ocean miles, including Melbourne to Hobart, Melbourne to Port Fairy, and Melbourne to Stanley races as helmsman.

Glenn Bourke, CEO Hamilton Island

Country:	Australia
Club:	Hamilton Island Yacht YC
When you started sailing:	Aged 11
Class started sailing in?	Manly Junior
Classes you have sailed?	Manly Junior, Flying Ant, Cherub, Moth, Flying Dutchman, Laser, Finn, Mumm 36, SB20, Admirals Cup – one tonner/two tonner, America's Cup – 12 metre/ACC, And many others
Currently sailing:	SB20

Sailing Achievements:

- 1977 2nd Moth Junior World Championships, Brisbane, AUS
- 1978 1st Australian Junior Moth Championship, Hobart, AUS
- 1980 1st Olympic Selection Flying Dutchman, Botany Bay, AUS
- 1987 1st America's Cup Defender Trials, Perth, AUS

- 1988 1st Australian Laser Championship, Belmont, AUS
- 1988 1st Pacific Laser Championship, Lake Taupo, NZL
- 1988 1st Belgian Laser Championship, Ostende, BEL
- 1988 1st Laser World Championship, Falmouth, GBR
- 1988 1st World 12 Metre Championship, Lulea, Sweden
- 1989 1st Australian Laser Championship – Mooloolaba, AUS
- 1989 1st Scandinavian Laser Championship, Ronneby, SWE
- 1989 1st Dutch Laser Championship, Workum, NED
- 1989 1st Laser World Championship, Aarhus, DEN
- 1989 NSW State Yachtsman of the Year
- 1989 Australian Yachtsman of the Year
- 1990 1st Australian Laser Championship – Perth, AUS
- 1990 1st Kiel Week Laser Class, Kiel, GER
- 1990 1st Dutch Laser Championship, Workum, NED
- 1990 1st French Laser Championship, Lorient, FRA
- 1990 1st, Laser World Championship, Newport, USA
- 1990 1st OK Dinghy Australian Championship, Balmain, AUS
- 1990 1st Finn Australian Championship, Botany Bay, AUS
- 1990 NSW State Yachtsman of the Year
- 1990 Australian Yachtsman of the Year
- 1991 1st Finn Australian Championship, Brisbane, AUS
- 1992 1st Olympic Selection Finn Class, Brisbane, AUS
- 1992 2nd Finn World Championship, Cadiz, SPA
- 1992 3rd Kiel Week Finn Class, Kiel, GER
- 1992 Olympics Finn Class
- 1993 1st Australian Laser Championship, Belmont, AUS
- 1993 2nd Admirals Cup (Australia) Cowes, GBR
- 1994 1st World Match Racing Championship, Perth, AUS
- 1995 3rd Mumm 36 World Championship, Solent, GBR
- 1995 1st World America's Cup Class Championship, San Diego,
- 1995 2nd Defender trials, America's Cup, San Diego, USA
- 1995 2nd Admirals Cup (Germany) Cowes, GBR
- 1996 1st Australian Laser Championship, Perth, AUS
- 1997 2nd Admirals Cup (Italy) Cowes, GBR
- 2003 1st 1720 European Championship, Howth, IRE
- 2003 1st 1720 UK Championship, West Mersey, GBR
- 2005 1st Laser SB3 UK Championship West Mersey, UK
- 2005 1st Laser SB3 European Championship, Lake Garda, ITA
- 2010 4th SB20 World Championship, Weymouth, GBR
- 2012 2nd SB20 World Championship, Hamilton Island, AUS
- 2015 1st SB20 Australian Championship, Tasmania, AUS
- 2015 3rd SB20 World championship, Lake Garda, ITA
- 2016 1st, SB20 Australian Championship, Blairgowrie, AUS

Mark Bulka

Country:	Australia
Club:	McCrae Yacht Club
When you started sailing:	Aged 5
Class started sailing in?	Sabot, Tiger Cub
Classes you have sailed?	Etchells, Finn, Contender, A Class, Sydney 38, Laser, Hydra, Maricat, Windrush, 16' Skiffs, Musto Skiff, SB20, Flying 15
Currently sailing:	Contender

Sailing Achievements:

Have won or placed in over 100 Australian and World Championships.

Some recent regattas of note:

- 2016 1st Contender World Championships, Santa Cruz, USA
- 2015 2nd Contender World Championship, Holland
- 2014 1st Contender World Championship, Sydney, Australia
- 2014 1st Contender Australian Championship
- 2013 1st Contender Australian Championship
- 2013 3rd Contender World Championships, Italy
- 2015 1st Contender Dutch National Championship
- 2013 1st Contender Kiel Week, Germany and 2nd 2015 Kiel Week
- 2016 1st SB20 Australian Championship

Also have Won Australian Championships in: Etchells, Finns and Sydney 38s.

Plus heaps of **State Championships** in: Contenders, Finns, Etchells, Sydney 38's, Hydra, Maricat, Impulse, Flying 15s, Windrush

Mat Belcher

Country:	Australia
Club:	Southport Yacht Club, RQYS, NRV.
When you started sailing:	Aged 7
Class started sailing in?	420
Classes you have sailed?	470, 420
Currently sailing:	470

Sailing Achievements:

- 2016 Silver medal, 470 class, Rio Olympics
- 2012 Gold Medal, 470 class, London Olympics
- 2011 and 2010 – Gold 470 World Championship
- 2011 and 2010 – Gold World Cup Championship
- 2011 – Silver at Olympic test event
- Gold in almost every Grade 1 Regatta in European and Oceania regions
- 2011 – QAS Athlete of the Year Finalist
- 2011, 2010, 2008, 2007 – Yachting Australia Sailor of the Year Finalist
- 2011 Jan, 2010, 2007 – Ranked World Number 1 in 470 Class
- QSport Queensland Athlete of the Year Finalist 2011
- 2010 – Rolex International Sailing Federation World Sailor of the Year Finalist
- 2010 – AIS Team of the Year Finalist
- 2004, 2000 – Gold & Silver 420 World Championship

Michael Coxon

Managing Director North Sails Australia.

Country:	Australia
Club:	CYCA, RSYS
When you started sailing:	At three weeks I am told, racing at five years with my sister in a Sabot
Class started sailing in?	Dinghy with table cloth set off an oar! First racing a Sabot.
Classes you have sailed?	Sabot, MJ, F11, 12-skiff then 18-skiff, RL24, Etchells, Farr 40, MC38, Maxi yachts
Currently sailing:	Etchells and yachts with clients

Sailing Achievements:

I do not really keep track but have won state, national, Interdominion championships across all the dinghy and skiffs listed above when I was a little younger.

I have won many Etchells championships as both skipper and crew sailing with the likes of Dennis Conner, John Bertrand and Iain Murray.

I was tactician and sailing master on Neville Creighton's maxi yachts *Shockwave* and *Alfa Romeo* for many years winning many long races and regattas including the Maxi Worlds, Hobart, Transpac, Fastnet race.

- 4 Admirals Cups representing Australia and Germany
- Have won the San Fran Big Boat series, Carbo Race, Kenwood Cup
- America's Cup as both Helmsman and Tactician with *Sydney '95*
- Lost the Farr40 Worlds on a countback, won the F40 Australian Champs
- 28 Sydney to Hobarts

Michael Quirk

Country:	Australia, Sydney
Club:	RPEYC Sydney
When you started sailing:	1985
Class started sailing in?	470, 505
Classes you have sailed?	International 505, Tasar, 470
Currently sailing:	International 505, Tasar

Sailing Achievements:

- 5 times Australian National 505 Champion
- 4th in 505 worlds
- 4th in Tasar Nationals
- 8th in Tasar Worlds

Mike Holt

Country:	United States (Born in GBR)
Club:	Santa Cruz Yacht Club
When you started sailing:	Before I could walk!
Class started sailing in?	Mirror
Classes you have sailed?	Mirror, 505, 49ers, Melges 24, Mumm 36
Currently sailing:	International 505

Sailing Achievements:

- 2009 – 2nd, SAP 505 worlds San Francisco, USA
- 2011 – 2nd, SAP 505 worlds Hamilton Island, AUS
- 2014 – 1st, SAP 505 worlds Kiel, Germany
- 2015 – 1st, SAP 505 worlds Pt Elizabeth, S Africa
- 2016 – 2nd SAP 505 worlds Weymouth, G. Britain
- 3-time UK 5O5 National Champion, 92, 14, 15
- 3rd US Sailing Champion of Champions, 2015

Noel Drennan

Country:	Born Ireland then Australia now USA
Club:	Royal Brighton YC, Sorrento Sailing Couta Boat Club
When you started sailing:	Aged 10
Class started sailing in?	National 12s in Dublin Mirror Dingy and Laser
Classes you have sailed?	Laser, Etchells, Farr 40, RC 44, TP 52, A class cat, Soling and have sailed many, many types of boats from Arabian Dow to the Version 5 AC boats
Currently sailing:	RC 44, Etchells, TP 52

Sailing Achievements:

- America's Cup four campaigns 2000 and 2003 with Stars and Stripes Dennis Conner
- 2007 and 2010 with BMW ORACLE including winning the America's Cup in 2010
- Volvo Ocean Race 2001 and 2005 winning in 2001 with Illbruck and Movistar in 2005
- Twice Australian champion in Etchells 1997 and 2001 Winning Victorian Etchells 5 times
- Olympic campaigns in Soling 1988 and 2000
- World Maxi boat winning twice
- RC 44 world championship winner 2012
- Sailed 31 Sydney to Hobart races winning overall twice and Line Honours three times.
- Starting working as apprentice sailmaker at Hood sails in Melbourne in 1980 and worked at North sails from 1984 to now.
- Many races all round the world giving a broad base of experience.

Rob Brown OAM

Development Manager Royal Motor Yacht Club, Broken Bay, NSW.

Country:	Australia
Club:	Royal Motor Yacht Club, NSW.
When you started sailing:	Aged 6
Class started sailing in?	Sabot
Classes you have sailed?	Sabot, 16-foot Skiff, 18-foot skiff, Etchells, Farr 40's, 12 metres, Melges 32, ½ Ton & 1 Ton.
Currently sailing:	Casual

Sailing Achievements:

- America's Cup Crew – *Australia II* – Winner 1983
- Admiral's Cup Winner 1979 – Australian Team *Impetuous*
- 10 Sydney to Hobarts,
- 18-foot skiffs – 3 World Championships
- 7 Grand Prix 18'Skiff Titles
- Australian & NSW Titles – Etchells – Open and Masters
- Australian Sporting Hall of Fame
- Caltex Sports Award
- Order of Australia Medal – Contribution to Sport
- AST Olympic Program Manager 2006–2008 Beijing Olympics

Sam Haines

Country:	Australia
Club:	Black Rock Yacht Club
Currently:	One design Manager – Australia – North Sails Sailmaker for 19 years
When you started sailing:	Aged 7
Class started sailing in?	Sparrow
Classes you have sailed?	Etchells, International 505 Dinghy, Sydney 38, Laser, OK Dinghy, J/24….
Currently racing:	Etchells

Sailing Achievements:

- 505 Junior World Champion

Some recent regattas of note:

- 2016 NSW State Titles (Etchells) 1st
- 2016 Gertrude Cup (Etchells – Cowes UK) 3rd
- 2016 World Championships (Etchells – Cowes UK) 6th

CHAPTER 1

Science of Sailing

CHAPTER 1

Science of Sailing

> *"Weight is only good in a steam roller."*
> **– Uffa Fox: 1898–1972**

Uffa was responsible for many of the developments which have contributed to the modern popularity of dinghy sailing. He first introduced the technique of planing to dinghy racing, and was influential in the introduction of trapezing.

THE SCIENCE AND PHYSICS OF SAILING

In order for us to improve our sailing results we first need to understand the science of sailing. What I have set out below is a precis of the knowledge that is out there, and is essential for us to grasp, if we wish to be mixing it with the best at the front of the fleet.

Some heavy stuff first, and then why understanding these laws is important to improving our results on the water.

Bernoulli's Law

This law explains lift in terms of high and low pressures on either side of the sail and centreboard or keel – as the wind hits the sails and the water molecules flow past the keel or centreboard, air particles and water molecules travel over each side.

The air moving across the outer side of the sail has a longer distance to travel in the same amount of time as the air moving across the inner side.

The same goes for water molecules flowing past your centreboard or keel.

Bernoulli's Law explains in part why a sailboat can sail almost in to the wind. The other part of the equation is the keel or centreboard which resists a lot of the lateral movement created by the sideways force of the wind on the sails.

The higher-velocity air on the outside of the sail forms a low-pressure area, and on the inside of the sail the slower air particles are packed together more densely and create a high-pressure area.

The difference in the pressure on the sail creates forward suction and produces lift, and this is what we are looking for to make our boat fast.

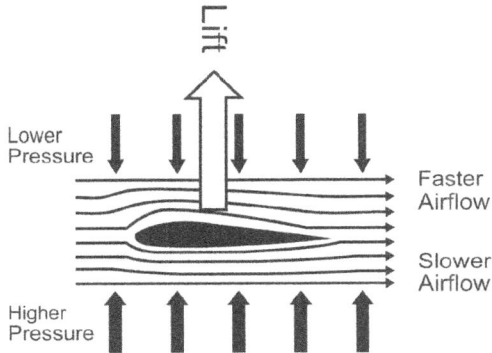

Newton's Third Law

Newton's Third Law describes lift in terms of the reaction of the wind's air particles to the mainsail and jib. The law states that every action has an equal and opposite reaction.

As the wind hits the sails from an opposing direction it generates drag, or backward pull.

If you look at lift from Newton's perspective, the movement of air creates an equal, opposite reaction or forward pull. It can also be applied to the interaction of the sails and the keel or centreboard.

The sails and the keel or centreboard create equal and opposite reactions to focus the boat's energy forward rather than sideways.

The keel or centreboard's main function is to keep the boat from being blown sideways in the wind (lateral resistance).

A lot is also happening underwater to help create lift – the keel or centreboard's broad, flat surface creates sideways force by displacing water in the opposite direction to which the boat is being pushed.

Although the keel or centreboard has a much smaller surface area than the sails, the density of the water allows it to initiate a force strong enough to cancel out the sideways force.

Newtons Third Law

Archimedes' Principle

Archimedes' Principle states that the upward buoyant force that is exerted on a body immersed in a fluid, whether fully or partially submerged, is equal to the weight of the fluid that the body displaces, and it acts in the upward direction.

The reason that this is important relates to making your boat as light as the class rules allow. Put simply, it will float higher and displace less water.

This neatly moves me to the importance of weight and sail boats.

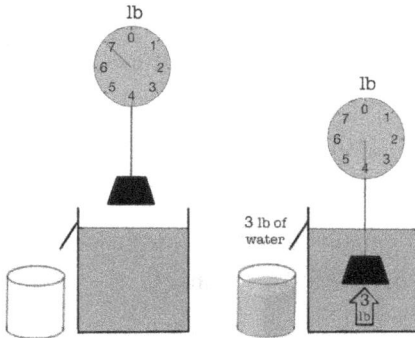

Archimedes' Principle

the buoyant force is equal to
the weight of the displaced water

lb

lb

3 lb of
water

Weight and Sailing

Weight slows a sailboat. A 4% increase in total weight (boat plus crew) decreases the downwind speed by about 1%.

A lighter boat will be faster.

1. The water's drag is equal in magnitude to the wind's force.

2. The drag is proportional to the submerged cross-sectional area of the hull.

3. The drag force is also proportional to the square of the boat speed.

4. The total drag force would stay the same if the speed decreased by 2% at the same time that the weight increased by 4%. This follows because a 2% decrease in boat speed corresponds to a 4% decrease in the square of the boat speed.

5. For downwind sailing, slower boat speed means an increased apparent wind speed. Combining the decreased boat speed with the increased apparent wind speed means the boat must slow by only about half as much (1%) when its weight is increased by 4%.

The Science of Sailing

There are essentially three forces that act on a sailing boat in the act of moving forward:

1. **Driving force:** Caused by the wind flowing across the sails. To make good use of this force, it is important to keep the sail at a small angle to the wind – this is why constant trimming is crucial for optimising the driving force.

2. **Sideways force:** When the wind presses into the sail it spreads not only into the forward-direction (driving force), but also sideways. It follows that the faster the boat is sailing, there is less sideways force.

3. **Heeling force:** is the force that the wind against the sail and causes resistance which is primarily provided by the keel or centreboard plus crew placement and weight.

You need to find the ideal trim for your sails and ideal crew placement in order to maximise the driving force, with minimised sideways and heeling force. Keeping your boat flat will also maximise the area of the centreboard and keel to resist sideways movement.

The Physics of Sailing

When you are standing still, you feel 'true wind', as soon as you move you feel 'airflow'.

The sum of the true wind and the wind felt through motion is called 'apparent wind'.

As a rule of thumb, most boats can sail at approximately 40 degrees to the wind at best.

In a fast boat, there's no point going straight downwind: you can never go faster than the wind, so you travel at an angle. If your boat is fast enough, then the relative wind always seems to be coming mainly from ahead of you.

This is the reason that boats like the 49er and the 18-footers never set ordinary spinnakers, they have asymmetrical sails that they can set even when they are travelling at small angles to the apparent wind.

How Boards and Keels (Foils) Work

The keel and centreboard are there in part to resist sideways forces when sailing upwind, and to generate lift when moving forward, not unlike an aircraft wing.

The lift is generated by water flowing over the surface so it is important to keep your boat moving forward efficiently otherwise lift will be lost. The greater the angle of attack the greater the lift, but there comes a point where the foil stalls.

The amount of lift is proportional to the square of the speed, so if you were to double the speed you would end up with four times the lift.

Drag is the bogey here though, and this increases in line with the angle of attack up to the stall point, which is in addition to the basic drag of the foils.

A stalled foil produces a lot more drag than when it is not stalled.

The lesson here is not to pinch too high, and keep the boat sailing as the more speed you can generate the more lift your foils will produce.

Translating Wind into Velocity

The forces around the mast are divided into driving force forward and force sideways. These two forces are expressed as vectors that sum up to a third force, being the force which moves the boat.

The movement occurs mostly forward, but also causes the boat to drift sideways.

This sideways movement is minimised through the use of the keel or centreboard, and by the placement of crew weight to keep the boat upright or flat.

Every boat has a centre of effort, a spot around which all forces act. Lots of boats can sail faster than the wind; they use relative wind speeds that occur when sailing at an angle to the wind. In that case, the friction between the hull and the water limits the speed of the boat.

The Importance of Preparation of Underwater Surfaces

A smooth underwater finish will reduce drag and increase speed.

A rough underwater surface creates frictional drag which is one of the factors that slows your boat. Other types of drag are wave making drag and trim drag. Trim drag can be remedied to a great extent by crew weight placement.

When the water flows past your hull, the water next to the hull (the boundary layer) ends up being carried along with the boat and is very thin – less than 50mm in most circumstances. Understanding the boundary layer is the key to how the hull surface roughness affects the performance of your boat.

The layer of particles just outside boundary layer is also dragged along with the boat, though not quite so fast. The next layer out is dragged along even less, and so on until at some distance out the water particles are not affected at all.

There are broadly speaking two types of flow inside the boundary layer – laminar and turbulent.

Laminar flow is when the water particles slip smoothly over one another. Laminar flow has much less drag than turbulent flow but it only exists on really smooth surfaces and at short distances from the bow or leading edge of the keel or centreboard in calm water.

Turbulent flow is when the water particles are moving around randomly. Inside this thin boundary layer of turbulent flow there is an even thinner layer of water, called the sub-layer. The sub-layer is really thin, typically the thickness of a human hair.

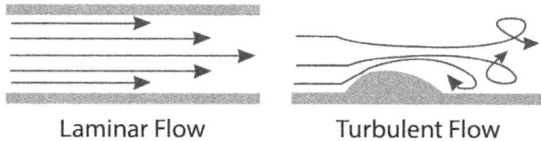

Laminar Flow   Turbulent Flow

If the roughness of the hull surface is high enough to protrude through the sub-layer, it will cause an increase in frictional drag which will slow you down. The more it protrudes, the more the friction.

The hull should be no rougher than the sub-layer thickness. The sub-layer thickness depends on the speed of the boat and how far back from the bow you are looking.

As you move back along the boat from the bow the sub-layer thickness increases, however, at any chosen point on the boat the sub-layer thickness decreases as boat speed increases.

The hull must be smoothest near the bow.

Hull Drag and Wave Making Resistance

A moving boat will experience hull drag, which is a function of underwater shape and skin friction. Clearly, the more 'skin', or wetted area, the greater the total frictional resistance, hence the need to sit forward in light air to reduce the wetted surface.

With your sails, it's a little more complicated. You need to imagine the centreboard/keel as a pivot point.

Sheet any sails in hard in front of this point and you will cause the boat to bear away.

Sheet any sails in hard behind this pivot point and the boat will round into the wind.

Therefore, if you ease jib and keep your main sheeted, the boat will round up. Conversely, a tight jib and an eased main means the boat should bear away.

So, if you have either of these combinations wrong you will need to counteract the directional pull with the rudder, which creates drag.

There are occasional times it may be better to use a lot of rudder though. As an example, in lumpy choppy conditions you can steer for the low point of each wave and the increased drag is more than compensated for by the reduced slamming.

Knowing what works comes from understanding the characteristics of your boat.

To give an example, a little windward heel as you turn in to a gybe, means you need less rudder, so less drag, a smoother turn and more speed.

At the bottom mark, some leeward heel, trim on mainsheet first, followed by jib sheet, will spin the boat up quicker and inside your competitors without the need for as much rudder movement. And as you pull on the last bit of jib sheet, you pull the boat flat with your body weight and you will accelerate quicker as well.

TAKEAWAYS

- Weight and its distribution can have an adverse effect on your boat speed, so make sure that your boat is as light as the class rules allow – a light boat will not have to displace as much water.

- Keep your boat as flat as possible to allow the keel or centreboard to project its largest flat surface and counteract sideways movement.

- We need to sand and polish the bottom of our boats to lessen drag, with the greatest concentration to the forward part of the hull.

- We don't need to know a lot about hydrodynamic theory, just remember – smooth is good in order to decrease wetted surface, and less resistance gives greater boat speed.

- In our manoeuvres, we need to move our body weight in such a way that we lessen the amount of steering needed to turn the boat, thus lessening drag created by the rudder.

- Increased boat speed gives you more lift from your keel or centreboard.

CHAPTER 2

Psychology and Mental Attitude

CHAPTER 2

Psychology and Mental Attitude

> *"Capsizes go hand in hand with 49er racing. I've had four or five capsizes in racing and still won the event."*
>
> **– Nathan Outteridge – 49er Gold Medallist and America's Cup Helmsman**

Psychology is perhaps one of the most neglected parts of sailing – it's always easier to mess around with your boat than with your mind. Working on your mental approach and the attitude you bring to the race is one of the most effective ways of improving your results.

INTERVIEW

I spoke with Gavin Dagley, Consultant Psychologist and World Laser Grand Master champion and I have copied excerpts from that discussion below. (For a full sailing summary for Gavin, see the Acknowledgment section at the front of the book.)

> **Q Brett: Do you think that it's psychology that has defeated a sailor who can win a race in a World Championship and the next day finish 50th?**

> **A Gavin:** I think the question typifies how people think about psychology in sport – that is, it's all about how do we deal with the anxiety, how we get our heads right, so that we can win. I believe that's the smaller part of the psychology of sailing. I think the really big part is how we learn. Sailing is may be the most cognitively complex sport there is. There are so, so many variables to deal with.
>
> You think about tennis. Tennis also has a lot of variables. That's true of every sport where your actions are a direct response to your competitor's actions. But imagine tennis where you had

30 other players on the court, and you had to adjust the string tension for every rally. Then you also have one person doing the grip, another doing the head speed and a third doing the direction of the shot.

I believe that the very best sailors are also the best learners. They might all have different approaches, but they learn fast. They are able to convert their experiences into tools and knowledge they can use on the course. That's what makes them good. I suspect it's also what helps manages their anxiety – that focus on "how do I do this better?"

Somehow, they're able to harness that in a way that allows them to focus on performing, whether they are winning or not.

So, that leads to the second part. Sailing is a performance. There's a whole lot of science behind it, but you've got to somehow turn that science into performance – what you do. Central to being able to make that translation is 'feel'. The very best sailors can feel what's going on – particularly with speed, but also with the wind, and with what is happening with the fleet.

Which leads to the third essential part – decision-making. How do I decide what to do in a particular situation? For instance, I've just sailed into a knock and so I want to tack – except, of course, if it's a persistent shift, when you hold on. But then you should "cross them when you can," but "the top mark is just over there, and I've got no runway left." How do I decide between all these priorities? It's at this point where people so often trip up with the anxiety stuff and start making bad decisions.

I think for the average sailor, or the club sailor who wants to improve, the anxiety stuff shouldn't be their focus of attention. The focus of attention should be on, 'how do I learn better and faster?' Make that the focus.

Q Brett: I was talking to a competitor in a Star regatta in the US and it involved one of the class champions who had a really bad first beat but had ended up finishing the race in second. Another competitor asked him how he had done it. He replied that he had settled down and reset.

A Gavin: The top people have the ability to reset. You talked earlier about being 'happy' in the boat – simply letting stuff go and focusing on enjoying the sail. Some people can do that. Some people can't. The good sailors can always reset somehow though – back into, "What am I going to do right now to get back to sailing this boat well?"

The hardest part, strangely, is knowing when a reset is needed. I would say a majority of people, when they're in the middle of a serious loss of focus, don't even know it's going on.

Q Brett: To indelibly etch what you have learned from both books and fellow competitors, you must practise. Is that why great sailors appear to get things right so effortlessly?

A Gavin: Time on the water is vital to build performance. There's just no other way around it. The more we do, the more we're going to learn. Along with the thinking, it is the only way to translate an experience into an idea, then, if it works, use it enough so that it is automatic.

Actually, there's a second way of practising, and that is doing the processing or review – be it debriefing or talking to experts or writing logbooks or whatever. You really want to try to get back into the moment – relive it if you like – and think through what happened and what else you could have done. It's a way of multiplying out one experience and getting the most from it.

When you are asking experts, one of the tricks is to listen for what they did, rather that the explanation of why – because the 'why' might not be right. Listen carefully for what they did and then try and explain it to yourself.

Gavin: I know attitude's a very loaded word. One of the most dangerous things is, "Oh, yeah. I know that already."

There are two ways to stop learning really quickly, one is to not practise or think and the other is to assume that I know that already.

Gavin: The good sailors can look further up the course than the not so good sailors. There's some really interesting psych studies, which they tried to determine decision-making ability with regard to tennis players.

They said, "So these people are our best decision-makers... Why are they better decision-makers? Have they got quicker reactions? Or have they got better vision?"

So, what they did was they set up a mock serving situation on video, a really good player served to somebody who was actually being tested, to test their response times and how they responded to a ball, to a serve.

What they found was there was no difference in visual acuity. There was no difference in motor speed. But the experts responded just a fraction earlier.

So, then they tested it again. They took out bits of the visual, to see which bits they were responding to.

The experts were able to notice things in the ball toss which gave them clues as to where the ball was going to go, whereas the less expert were watching the flight of the racquet head to know where the ball was going to go.

I think that that's a really powerful story, because what happens is that you watch the really good sailors and they'll say, "I know this is going to happen and this is going to happen, this is going to happen".

They've got more time to make those decisions. I'm not sure whether they force it or they just do it intuitively, but they look further up the track and can see how it's going to unfold.

That comes back to the learning thing. So the learning process has a number of components to it. And one of the biggies is to actually rethink what's going on, because then when I see that circumstance again, I'm actually much more clued up as to what's going on.

FROM OTHER SOURCES

Mind Sailing

- In one-design racing, your equipment is the same as everyone else's, there are only two ways to beat your opponent – through superior physiology (your size, weight and fitness) or through superior psychology (just about everything else!).

- Learning new mental skills will do you more good than buying some fancy new piece of equipment. These skills once obtained never wear out, and cost you nothing.

Performance Psychology

- Are there particular opponents who you consistently lose to but have no business beating you?

- You must not believe that a fellow competitor is better than you. If he is currently sailing a little faster than you, you need say to yourself that this is only happening at this moment, soon it will be my turn to be faster.

- When lining up against practice partners or other competitors sail your hardest and you can bet that your fellow competitors may get a complex about you.

Mental Toughness – Mental Stamina

- Many psychologists think that mental practise is as important as actual practise.

- Mental toughness is the common denominator of all successful sailors and has given them the strength to stay in control and survive every problem thrown at them.

- Sailors who are mentally tough and fit, give their best when pushed to the brink.

- Success in sailing is as much about mental toughness as it is about competence and hard work. Mental toughness is what keeps you going and gets you pumped.

- Mental toughness gives you an edge that enables you to be consistent during a race or regatta, it enables you to stay confident and strong minded during high-pressure situations.

- Much of mental toughness is simply attitude and self-esteem. If you are mentally tough, giving up is never an option and when faced with difficulties on the race course you are able to focus on finding a solution to the problem, whether it be a problem with your boat or a fellow competitor.

Concentration

- You must try to put past achievements out of your mind and you must concentrate on the race that you are in now.

- Concentration is one of the two key processes for sailing, but concentration on what? Concentration has to be directed at something.

- Speed is usually the first thing to go when sailors get anxious. When concentration flags you start looking around at everything except the basics of what makes your boat go fast – steering well, trimming well, and using your body weight to maximum effect.

- Unlike other athletes, sailors not only have to think about their equipment but also have to consider the state of their playing field. The sea is in a constant state of change due to wind, waves and tide. To remain at the top of their game, a sailor must consider all variables and this requires a huge amount of concentration.

- Sailing is one of the most complex sports in the world owing to the amount of concentration and information processing needed to sail optimally.

- Concentration is about relaxing and identifying what is important to focus your attention on and maintaining that focus. You must recognise when your concentration shifts to irrelevant things and be able to bring it back to what's important.

- Concentration is a skill that is central to performance. Good or bad performances are often attributed to a sailor's ability to concentrate.

- Everyone loses concentration at some point while sailing. The skill is to be aware when this is happening and minimise the time you are not totally focused.

Building and Maintaining Confidence

- Do you regularly perform better in practise than you do at the big regattas? Bring your practise confidence to the race track.

- Many times we have let an opponent past because we think he is better than us.

- Remember you paid the same entry fee as everyone else, have put in the same effort to be there as they have, so have the same right to success as they do.

Attitude and Control

- Many sailors can get a complex about you and a simple thing like sailing hard on the run or beat out to the course will show others that you are a force to be reckoned with.

- You must always keep your spirits up and, if you are hurting after a long beat just remember so are your fellow competitors.

- If you are behind in the fleet and you are tired and hurting, remember so are the guys in front of you.

Effects of Stress

- Repeating the same mistakes

- Frustration

Dealing with Negatives

Quite often the best way to deal with negatives is to focus on a positive and to use a relaxation technique that works for you in order to forget about the negative emotions.

Never start using excuses as to why you lost a race or lost places during a race. What has happened can never be changed so there is no point dwelling on it.

Most great sailors use relaxation techniques to refocus when something has gone wrong out on the course.

One technique is to take a number of deep breaths which has a calming effect or some sailors merely use a word that they say to themselves such as "focus" or "concentrate" to reset their mind to the job of winning the yacht race.

Learn to Stay Calm and Composed Under Pressure

Prior to going out on the course to race, at least 90% of your efforts are in preparation, practise and working on your fitness, with 10% being mental. Once at the start line the percentages are reversed.

One of the reasons for the best sailor's success is overcoming negativity and self-doubts.

Part of the technique for achieving this is to focus on the right things and don't allow negative thoughts such as "I am not as good as the other guys" or "I am rubbish in light winds" to preoccupy your thinking.

Concentrate on what you are trying to achieve, don't dwell on mistakes you have made, but rebound quickly by thinking about the next phase of the race.

Mentally Prepare for Races

When speaking to champion sailors a common theme regarding their success is preparation. Having your mind right is right up there with physical fitness.

Whilst you are training physically leading up to an event, think about what you are exercising for, and think about being out on the course, mentally rehearsing situations that you will encounter, including stressful events, and how you might tackle them, working through outcomes and strategies.

Talk with your crew and fellow competitors regularly leading up to the event in order to get your mind in the right space and distant from day to day life stresses.

TAKEAWAYS

- The best sailors are the best learners.

- The best sailors feel what is going on.

- To be a great sailor you must be a good decision maker.

- Develop the ability to reset to happy when something goes wrong.

- When debriefing with sailors after a race listen to what they did, not the explanation, then note what they did and try to explain it to yourself.

- Never give up.

- Concentration above all else is paramount if you are to win yacht races consistently.

- Practise mentally as much as you practise physically.

- Build and maintain confidence.

- Learning mental skills is more important than spending money on the latest fancy piece of equipment.

CHAPTER 3

Sailing Fitness and Diet

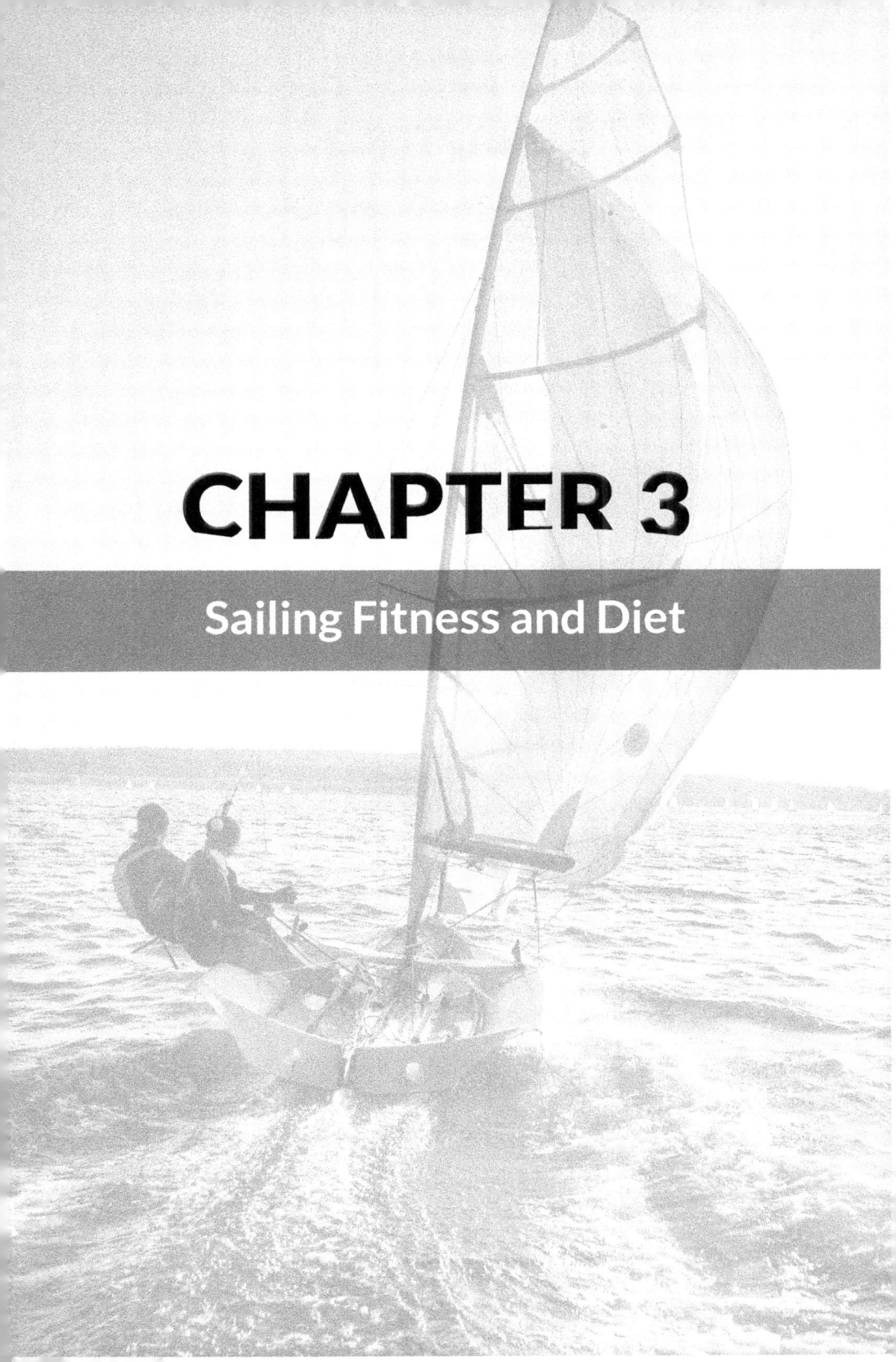

CHAPTER 3

Sailing Fitness and Diet

> *"You can no longer just be a good sailor. You have to be an incredible athlete as well. Having said that, you can be a great athlete, the strongest guy in the world, but if you can't anticipate and make decisions under stress and exhaustion and think ahead, then you won't be able to cut it, either."*
>
> **– James Spithill (Australian), two times winning America's Cup Helmsman, Oracle Team USA, and multiple World Champion in various classes.**

SAILING FITNESS

Be Scientific

- It's important to keep records of your fitness. The aim is to find out what works through trial and error.

- Body weight is the first thing you should keep track of over the long term. Find out what is the optimum weight for your chosen class.

- Think of tests you can apply to yourself to measure your fitness for sailing.

- Use an excel spreadsheet to keep results, from time trials in cycling, rowing machine, pool running and even surf ski paddling as part of your fitness regime to gauge your improvement.

Fitness Goals and Goal Setting

Several key principles can be applied to help you set your physical activity goals. These include:

- Pinpoint your ultimate goal and find out how to achieve it.

- Set small, specific mini-goals.

- Monitor your progress regularly.

- Adapt to changing circumstances.

- Don't be too hard on yourself

Be realistic – Your ultimate fitness goal could be to be fit enough to participate in a competition on a set date. Whatever you decide, make the goal realistic.

Remember that most of us will never be world-famous athletes or supermodels – think about what is achievable for you and write down your goals.

Be specific – Don't make your ultimate goal a general statement like, 'I want to lose weight'. Make it measurable, write down exactly how many kilograms you want to lose.

Choose a goal that is meaningful and important to you, not to anybody else.

Find Out How to Achieve Your Ultimate Fitness Goal

Once you have decided on your health and fitness goal, you need to consider how you will reach that goal. Different fitness goals require different approaches.

For example, weight loss requires you to regularly burn more kilojoules than you consume, and some of us need a personal trainer to be accountable to.

An effective strategy may include:

- Choose aerobic activities such as walking.

- Get a program for fitness designed by a professional.

- Get an eating plan designed by a professional.

- Exercise for at least 30 minutes on all or most days of the week.

- Cut back on junk food.

- Eat smaller food portions.

Increase the amount of fresh fruits and vegetables, lean meats, low-fat dairy products and wholegrain foods in your daily diet.

Set Small, Specific Fitness Goals

You are more likely to reach your ultimate goal if you break it down into short-term mini-goals. Short-term goals are specific daily actions or behaviours that lead you to your ultimate goal.

Suggestions include:

- Know your starting point, so you can pick activities that are comfortable and realistic for you, and build slowly at a pace that feels right for you.

- Set a reasonable timeframe. For example, if you want to lose 20 kg, then a realistic weight loss of 1 kg of body fat every one to two weeks means that you need to allow yourself around 20 to 40 weeks.

- Consider your exercise routines as mini-goals. A mini goal might be to exercise on all or most days of the week. The more mini-goals you achieve, the more motivated you will become.

If you are unsure how to best achieve your particular fitness goals, ask an expert. See your doctor, or consult an exercise physiologist, physiotherapist or appropriately qualified and certified personal trainer.

Sailing Fit Exercises

Upper Body/Core:	Legs/Core:
• Rowing Machine • Stretching • Lat Pulldowns • Upright Rows • Triceps Extensions • Bicep Curls • Shoulder Shrugs • Hanging Knee Raises • Hiking Bench (full extension/ touch toes) • Planks	• Elliptical Treadmill (Cardio) 30 mins, • Stretching • Leg Press/Squats • Leg Extensions • Lunges with Weights in Each Hand • Hiking Bench (full extension/ touch toes) • Hanging Knee Raises

The Five Most Effective Exercises for Sailing Training Are:

1. Chin-ups

2. Squats

3. Interval training – alternating bursts of high and low intensity activity

4. Partner exercises – train with a person of similar abilities and strength to push each other harder

5. Team challenges and competition – teams working towards one objective

Please note: It is my suggestion to get a proper program from a qualified sports personal trainer and get them to monitor your progress.

Don't wing it, as you may do more harm than good.

Relaxing and Recovery Techniques

You don't get fitter from training until you get a chance to rest and let the body rebound.

You can recover faster for your next training session using recovery strategies like remedial massage or, if you want to go a little more hard-core, you could try cold water immersion, many athletes use rivers, the bays or ocean for this.

While getting in is hard, afterwards you really feel a difference by way of reduced soreness and faster recovery.

Sleep

Physical conditioning and good nutrition are critical in reaching peak athletic performance, and sleep plays an equally important role.

It's become clear that the quality and quantity of sleep obtained by elite sailors can be the edge between winning and losing on race day.

Five areas that sleep has the greatest impact on are –

- Improved reaction time – sleep deprivation significantly reduces reaction times

- Injury rates are reduced

- Longer sailing career

- Crucial to the body's physiological, biochemical and cognitive restoration

- Fewer mental errors – sleep loss impairs judgement

Training

Training for sailors should include 'dry land' and 'on water' training. Dry land training should include at least three fitness/cardiovascular sessions per week in addition to strength training sessions.

We must also train on the water, and these can be technical sessions with a coach, solo skill improvement practice or race-style sessions with a training partner.

The frequency of on water training will vary depending on time commitments, availability of people and of course weather.

Fitness doesn't happen overnight, so take advantage of the 'off season' and winter months to get in shape for summer when it really starts blowing.

Not only will you look and feel better, but you'll also notice a big improvement in your sailing.

Preparing for Action

- It is important to dial back your workouts leading up to a big regatta

- Do shortened routines and focus on cardio leading up to an event

- There's no point to being worn out from a hard week at the gym before the regatta starts

Muscular Fitness

- The difference between muscular and cardiovascular fitness is that a limitation of oxygen being supplied to the muscles will occur in cardiovascular fitness

- In muscular fitness, the oxygen to the muscles is not being decreased, but the muscles are simply not able to continue contracting. The more times a muscle is able to contract without becoming fatigued, the better the muscular fitness

- Muscular fitness is nearly as important as cardiovascular fitness to ensure that the muscles are able to endure long periods of contractions

The Importance of Stretching

- Stretching is just as important as exercise, it helps improve flexibility and increases your range of motion

- Stretching assists correct posture by lengthening tight muscles that pull areas of the body away from their intended position

- Stretching has the potential to decrease injury by preparing muscles for work before activity

- Stretching increases blood and nutrient supply to muscles, thereby possibly reducing muscle soreness

- Even a short amount of time (10–15 minutes) of stretching can calm the mind, provide a mental break, and give your body a chance to recharge

- Classes like yoga or Pilates offer you a chance to spend an hour releasing tension physically and mentally.

DIET

Hydration

Dehydration is common in sailing due to the length of time spent on the water and subsequent exposure to environmental conditions, and even mild dehydration can impair skill and judgment when competing in a yacht race.

Water – Hands down, water is the best option unless you are a heavy sweater. When you sweat you lose salt, if this is you a combination of water and a sports drink may be the answer.

Sports Drinks – are a good idea if your race or workout goes for more than an hour, they contain sodium, potassium and chloride.

Choose one that has no artificial colours and other additives such as vitamins, minerals and too many calories.

Sports drinks provide fuel to help maintain blood glucose levels during racing, plus they contain higher levels sodium an essential electrolyte which is responsible for controlling the total amount of water in the body and is important for controlling blood volume and maintaining muscle and nerve function.

Make sure there is minimal sugar – be wary of sports drinks that are loaded with sugar.

NOTE: Drinks with high sugar content will actually cause your body to become dehydrated and make you thirstier.

What We Need to Eat – Basic Nutrition

Eating like an athlete is just as important as training like one. Stay away from sugar and processed foods. Eat plenty of complex carbs, veggies, and protein. Fish, eggs and chicken are great protein sources and low in fat.

Before a regatta eat plenty of carbs, get a good sleep, and then eat lots of small snacks during the course of racing.

Apples, wholegrain bread, protein bars, and peanut butter are great fuel for your body.

Although you might not feel like it, force yourself to drink a little in between races and get a snack.

Training and Racing Diet

Most sailors juggle work or other commitments in conjunction with the demands of training.

The best advice for any sailor is to plan ahead and to ensure the body is sufficiently fuelled before, during and after all training sessions and races.

Ready access to food and fluid is crucial when training and racing. Portable, nutritious options should be carried on the boat for easy access while on the water.

Some good options include:

- Sandwiches

- Cereal or muesli bars

- Sports bars or gels

- Fresh fruit or dried fruit and nut mix

- Sports drink

- Water

TAKEAWAYS

- Be scientific about your fitness and keep records.
- Set goals and make them small, specific and achievable.
- Get a fitness program custom designed for you by a professional.
- Make sleep an important part of your training.
- Don't neglect stretching as part of your program.
- Watch what you eat both on and off the water and avoid processed
- Foods. It is advisable to get an eating plan designed by a professional
- Understand the importance of hydration and always carry plenty of fluids when out training or racing.

CHAPTER 4

Planning

CHAPTER 4

Planning

> *"If you fail to plan, you are planning to fail."*
> — **Benjamin Franklin**

Crew Travel

This takes the form of air or land by car depending where the regatta is.

If you need to travel by air book early to get the best deals and remember you need to get to the regatta venue from the airport, so plan whether you need to hire a car or whether there is adequate, reliable public transport.

Extra cost here gives you less money to spend on your boat and entertainment.

If travelling by car in your own country, allow for holiday traffic and make sure your vehicle is up to the journey.

Transport and Logistics for Boat

Don't forget the trailer, paying special attention to lights, registration and wheel bearings if you are travelling interstate.

If you haven't attended regattas and championships overseas, have a chat to someone who has. There is an enormous amount of effort required to transport your boat, yourself and crew.

Think carefully about spares and tools that you will need whilst at a regatta, you can't always rely on the local chandlery having what you want or a fellow competitor having the tools you may need.

Getting the paperwork right in the beginning ensures that the return of your boat after the regatta goes smoothly and limits the extra costs and painful communication that comes from poor planning.

Finding a company who have transported boats overseas is essential and the old adage of check, check and check again cannot be stressed too heavily when it comes to rules and regulations.

Accommodation

Make sure that you plan this early – soon after entering makes a lot of sense. You are going any way so no need to hold off.

Regattas are regularly in the high tourist season and accommodation not only gets scarce but also becomes more expensive as you get closer to the time.

The best stuff gets taken early and good, close by and comfortable digs are very important.

Comfort is especially true if you have had a bad day on the course and need to regroup or if it has been tough out there and you need a good night's sleep.

If you have a car, make sure parking is available nearby. I have been to regattas in tourist destinations where up to an hour has been spent when arriving back at the accommodation looking for somewhere to park.

It can make sense to share with other crews doing the regatta, many an "aha!" moment has come around the dinner table when discussing the days races.

It's a great time and place to debrief with other crews. In many instances they may have been struggling with the same issues as you.

People

- **Crew** – Make sure that you and your team have sailed together as much as possible in varying conditions prior to the regatta.

  If your regular crew can't attend, get to the regatta venue as early as possible and train hard with the replacement. On the water, try to have a training partner and hone your skills with them.

  There is no substitute for time in the boat together.

- **Support** – If you are in a position to have someone to assist with shore-based activities, this leaves you and your crew nothing to do but to concentrate on the sailing.

  A person to pick up spares and attend to repairs is invaluable.

Other things that they can do to enable you to concentrate on the sailing are attending to paperwork, checking notices, and presenting the boat for measurement, chasing up weather reports and local knowledge.

Each day the support member can go over the checklist and remedy anything that is awry, making sure that food and water are on board and the myriad of other things that take your focus away from the racing.

- **Coach** – Never underestimate the value of a coach, even better still one that can attend the regatta. As a minimum have someone who can help you work up to the regatta with drills and advice to get you honing your technique and get you going fast.

  If you can have a coach at the regatta they can watch you sailing prior to the start and offer constructive advice such as settings and information on what is happening around the course prior to the start.

  A coach can watch the race as it develops and give constructive feedback on what you could do to improve.

Pre-regatta Training or Warm-up Regattas

If you are able, attend regattas at the club that the championship is going to be sailed.

If that is not possible attend events in the country or hemisphere that the event will be held, even months out such as national championships or other well attended regattas.

If you can't get your boat there for these events prior to the championship, charter – this will enable you to see what the standard of racing is like and who you need to beat.

Attending pre-event regattas may show you what aspects of your sailing you need to practise to be fully prepared when you arrive at the main event.

A word of warning though if chartering – make sure the boat is up to the latest spec and that the gear is top-notch. I have seen charter boats which have needed constant repairs during the regatta or have had sails that were well beyond their use-by date.

If you are bringing your own sails to use on a chartered boat, ensure that they are cut to suit the mast and set up that the boat you are using has.

I have seen sailors who have performed above expectations by attending a number of regattas prior to the main event.

Finance

Ensure you have allowed enough money to cover food and entertainment at the regatta. Most of us finance our own sailing but if you are well connected don't discount talking to friends and colleagues about a bit of financial assistance.

Assistance doesn't need to be only cash and could be clothing, travel, accommodation or equipment. All some people want in return is some photos and regular communication about results, the venue and so on.

Constantly worrying about money will weigh on your mind and affect your sailing performance so make sure you are adequately funded.

Goal Setting for a Regatta

You should enter every regatta with a goal, of course to win is the ultimate but perhaps your goal is to finish further up the leader board, to beat certain fellow competitors or to simply improve certain aspects of your boat handling or boat speed.

Goals need to be specific and measurable and writing them down, even on the boat, will help with your focus. A goal could be as simple as acquiring a certain personal weight, be it up or down, by the time the event starts.

The goals you set must be realistic but not too easy either otherwise the sense of achievement is diminished. If you set too tough a goal and don't achieve it, it can lead to disappointment and the desire to give it away.

You should keep a list of goals and tick them off as you achieve them, but be prepared to add others to the list.

Administration

- **Develop a checklist** – This only needs to be done once and a good checklist will get continually modified from experience the more regattas you do. If you are uncertain, have a chat with someone who has travelled before and make notes.

- **Entry** – Get this out of the way early, there is no point paying a late entry fee and in most cases this is the first thing you do, this then triggers booking flights and accommodation.

- **Insurance** – Your boat will most probably be insured in your home territory but it's worth making sure you are covered interstate, on the road and overseas. If your boat is being transported out of the country, you will need additional cover. Take proof of insurance with you as the regatta organiser will need to see this when you check in at the registration desk.

- **Paperwork** – Make sure you are aware of customs and quarantine requirements and that you get advice from a freight forwarder who has had experience in sending boats away to overseas regattas. This will save a lot of heartache and expense when your boat returns.

- **Weighing and measurement** – Don't overlook the importance of this, make sure that you travel with your measurement certificate and before your boat leaves home ensure that all safety equipment complies with the class rules.

  At many regattas I have attended there has been a mad scramble to buy things like the right size and length tow rope, provide a towing ring or have the right size paddle.

Time and Money Management

Arrive with enough time to settle in to your accommodation, locate the local supermarket, chandler and places to eat after hours.

Make sure that you have a couple of days up your sleeve to get out on the course and familiarise yourself with the sailing area and access to the course.

Don't arrive with no spare cash – there is nothing worse than putting in all the effort and cost to get there and then find that a bit of broken gear means that you have to miss races.

Play to Your Strengths, Minimise Your Weaknesses

In your planning, you should continually reappraise your strengths and weaknesses and training should focus on those things that you are not good at. As an example, gybing in heavy air and big seas.

It may mean a few swims but go out on an ugly day and practise those gybes.

TAKEAWAYS

- Once you decide to go to a regatta book your airfares straight away, they rarely get cheaper as the time approaches.

- As with booking airfares, book accommodation as soon as you decide to go to an event, the best stuff gets taken first.

- Where possible, attend lead up regattas and if the main event is overseas try to race in that hemisphere prior to your regatta.

- To get the most out of a regatta set goals and make them realistic.

- As part of your planning, develop a checklist for each aspect such as logistics (boat and travel), spares, administration (entry, insurance etc.)

- Try not to go to a regatta underfunded, worry about money concerns will sap your energy and ruin your concentration.

- Work with a coach and if at all possible have him or her attend the regatta with you.

CHAPTER 5

Preparation

CHAPTER 5

Preparation

> *"My golden rules are, preparation, practise and fitness. If you don't have all three you will be leaving numbers on the table. You won't beat me unless you have done at least as well in all three. I know I will be better in at least two! If you have all three you will have the confidence to race under your terms and you know that, bad start, bad tack or any other problem will be overcome over the course of a race and an event.*
>
> **– Mike Holt, USA, twice 505 world champion and twice runner up.**

INTERVIEW

I spoke with Sam Haines just after he returned from the 2016 Etchells world championships at Cowes in the UK about their preparation.

Q Brett: Do you write down a lot of the settings that worked after each race?

A Sam: Not particularly. We would set up our tuning for the venue and log that a week out from a Worlds and for a Nationals, it might be two days.

Obviously, with venues that you've sailed at before, you've got prior understanding of the venue, but through the regatta we keep to our tuning guide.

Q Brett: Can you give us a bit of background on how you prepared for the 2016 worlds Etchells regatta?

A Sam: We actually went to the venue about six weeks prior to the event and were there for 12 days. We did one event and then did a few days of training with some of the other boats that we did the Worlds with.

During that time –

1. You check in with the venue.

2. You know where you're going to eat your dinner at night.

3. You know where your house is.

There's a lot in a regatta preparation. After those 12 days we came back to Australia for a couple of weeks and caught up with family life, business and so on.

We then went back for ten days prior to the Worlds. We did four days of intense coaching then had a day off the boat and didn't go near the water.

Then we're into the Europeans and the Worlds, so it was quite a long-winded exercise, but there's no substitute for the variety. You don't win the regatta on the last day.

Brett: How important is practise time, and of that practise, what percentage of that do you actually go and practise on your own rather than with another boat?

Sam: We did, I would say, 80% of our lead up to the Worlds by ourselves just working on technique. We were confident that our boat speed was pretty good, and then of that time, we made sure that we would line up with one of the better teams, just doing a short up wind. Maybe only ten minutes at the end of the session and just check in.

We all do enough racing to actually do the boat-on-boat stuff.

One thing I will say with the training though is that you want to do it in not short sessions but reasonably short sessions.

If you have to go out for a whole day you're not going to achieve anything apart from boredom.

Q **Brett – Sure that's a good point. So what you're saying is more sessions rather than long days on the water?**

A **Sam:** More sessions but short sessions. When I say short, anything over two and a half hours is a long session.

You need to go out there with a purpose, have a goal, and go and achieve that goal, That goal might take you two and a half hours to achieve or it might take you a half hour to achieve. But tick the box and move on.

Don't go out there and say – All right, now we're just going to go and do a couple of tacks – you need to have a goal, achieve it, tick the box and come in.

You might find that those days that you got the box ticked in an hour or so, you come back in and that's the day that you do your boat work.

Q **Brett: Do you try and mix it up with conditions as well? Should you go out on a really light day for instance and should you also go on a day when it's pretty crappy, like really hard?**

A **Sam:** Yeah, that's a good point but again, over at the Worlds sometimes prior to the event we went out at 8:30 or 9:00 in the morning to get light breeze. We also went out later in the day to get some real heavy breeze.

The problem is if you don't practise in light air, when it goes light you don't have the setting for your boat and you fall of the edge.

Q **Brett: I noticed that you guys have spent a lot of time getting your boat just right. And having easy to operate systems, tweaking and getting things right. Have you found that's been an important part of why you guys have improved?**

A **Sam:** I think there's two parts to that. And one is that with preparation, you know that everything works 100%. You need to have gone out and tested that six months prior to the event.

There's also the other side of it, and that is having that set up for the people you've got on the boat.

At the Worlds, we had a new person on the bow of the boat. Previously I was doing the bow and had it set up the way that works for me, but our new guy wanted to change a few things to suit his style and move a couple of the control lines to different positions – remember that the boat is a tool.

So you make it custom to the people using it and you have to set up the boat to what works for the people in the boat not to what somebody says this is how your Etchells or your 505 have to be set up.

Q Brett: What are some common tuning mistakes you see crews make when it comes to preparation?

A Sam: You get to the venue, you don't have your boats tuning guide written out.

Every boat is slightly different and the way that you sail it is slightly different. Set up your chart.

Again, at the Worlds I spent, probably an hour's exercise at the end of each day's training, once we were happy with what we had scribbled out in pencil, to neatly document that, print it, put it on the side of the boat and know what that tuning guide was. Not "Oh, yesterday we had this setting".

Q Brett: Teams should have it written down and visible on the boat.

A Sam: Yeah, laminate it and stick it on the side of the boat. If you are a bit off on the day you're racing, and we all do it, we're humans, so one day you might have been on the phone to home and something's gone bad or someone on the boat is not feeling 100% because they got the cold that's going around the boat park or whatever so you're not asking "Ah, what was that setting again?"

You don't need to remember that stuff. It's all written down.

Brett – Thanks Sam for your valuable insights in to preparation.

FROM OTHER SOURCES

Pre-race and Venue Homework

Get hold of any history of past events at the venue, plus any information that the conducting club may have about weather and expected conditions.

Go to the weather bureau and get history for the area.

Speak to sailors from your class who have this venue as their home club or who have sailed there on a number of occasions.

Boat, Sails, Gear Preparation Checklist

Many times the outcome of a race is as dependent on what you have done prior to the race as to what you do out on the course. Sometimes no matter how good your tactics and strategy are a simple breakage could render all that useless.

- Hull – make sure that your hull is well sanded and polished, centreboard strips are in good condition, venturis if fitted are working efficiently, buoyancy tanks are dry and there are no extraneous pieces of kit in your boat which adds unwanted weight.

- Update any gear that looks tired or worn especially control lines.

- Mast, boom and poles – check that all halyards, stays and trapeze wires are not worn or damaged and that pins are secure, knots tight and that anything that can tear a sail or injure flesh is taped. Mark the full hoist position on all halyards.

- Deck hardware – check all cam cleats for spring tension and tape anything that may cause a sail tear or cut legs hands and arms. Check the length of all sheets and control lines and shorten anything that is too long. This not only reduces weight but also minimises clutter. Have marks on sheets and stick or draw numbers and reference scales for the jib tracks, outhaul and halyards so that you can easily duplicate settings that you know are fast in various conditions.

- Centreboard and rudder – ensure that all nicks and gouges are filled and sanded and the surfaces are polished and most importantly that rudder safety clips are working.

- Sails – select the correct battens for the day's forecast.

- Write on the deck, with a china graph pencil, things like the starting sequence, courses, tide times and anything else that will remind you to sail fast.

- Tools and spares – carry a shackle key with screwdriver head on your person along with some spare shackles and short lengths of rope or different diameters. A tool like a Leatherman can be very useful to deal with unexpected breakages that can occur even in the best prepared boat.

Self

- Physically peaking at the right time –Have a program leading up to the regatta that has you aerobic fitness at its peak and muscles where you need them to be to enable you to sail the whole event without the need to let up for a rest.

- Body and weight – most classes have an optimum weight range for the position that you sail in. Be as near as you can to this weight, this will have a major effect on how your boat performs in a variety of conditions.

- Clothing on water – adequate wetsuit and clothing for the area that you are sailing, don't underestimate the time on the water and you may be returning on dark when it may be considerably colder than during the race.

- Clothing off water – don't neglect after hours both early mornings and evenings. Think about the temperatures but also social activities and presentation nights. It pays to take a range of gear and remember, heaven forbid you may need to work in to the night to repair a broken boat or rig.

Goal Setting

There a number of goals you should set with regards to your sailing. The first relates to your calendar for the season, be realistic about your time, resources and your ability.

Setting goals means you are likely to end up sailing more and having more fun.

The second relates to your competitiveness, you should always be aiming for the next rung on the ladder and should work out what it takes to get there and then go about achieving each goal, a number of small achievements will culminate in the ultimate prize.

Goal setting is a skill and a way to bring structure and discipline to your learning and improvement, plus it builds and assists with maintaining confidence.

Mental Preparedness

In the lead-up to the event, try to do something every day with regard to your sailing and this will help your mind to slowly eliminate outside influences.

It goes without saying that you should eliminate any mental problems from your mind before the races, this includes work, personal and family issues.

You should arrive at the regatta venue well rested and with time to get your mind settled in at the venue and be thinking only of the races ahead of you.

Try not to involve yourself in ongoing work problems and if at all possible, don't contact the office until the regatta is finished.

Checklists

a) Develop a checklist for all the essential things like sailing instructions, chart of the sailing area, measurement certificate, relevant membership cards, and proof of insurance.

b) Create a boat and spares checklist especially if travelling interstate or overseas and this includes practice sails, spare equipment (mast, replacement fittings, nuts bolts, screws and washers) tools, glues, safety equipment, silicones and polishes.

c) Personal gear which includes wetsuits, life jacket, gloves, boots, hat, and miscellaneous clothing items, sunglasses and sunscreen

d) Miscellaneous items including water bottles, food etc.

The list varies from competitor to competitor and boat to boat and is something that each of us needs to build for ourselves – the outline above is a starting point only.

Day of the Race

- Check and print out the weather forecast and tide information.

- Select the sails – if the class rules allow more than one set, select the right sails for the forecast conditions, if you have the luxury of a coach and coach boat and make sure they have your spare sails out on the water.

- Make sure you have sunscreen, sunglasses, gloves and a hat.

- Set mast rake and shroud tension – depending on how difficult your boat is to adjust, in some cases it makes sense to set your rake for the day's event prior to leaving the beach based on the forecast. If your rake is easily adjusted leave that for part of your pre-race drills.

- Food and drink – purchase and pack food for the time on the water and relevant drinks be it water or sports drinks.

- Check the regatta notice board – there is nothing worse than arriving at the race course with a plan only to find that there has been a change to the sailing instructions and that the change was posted on the event notice board.

- Get on the course at least an hour before the start – when you arrive at the course early it allows you to work out what the wind is doing and to tune your boat for the conditions.

- It is essential to have a tuning partner because trying to work out whether you have your boat going at optimum on your own is close to impossible.

TAKEAWAYS

- Have all your settings recorded, printed on a laminated sheet and placed in a visible place on the boat.

- Part of preparation is organising good accommodation, locating places to eat and locating the availability of supplies.

- Get to the regatta early and where possible attend a regatta prior to the main event.

- Do pre-race and venue homework.

- Have a travel and regatta checklist so that nothing gets forgotten.

- Get yourself in physical shape so that you are at your peak at the regatta.

- Set goals for the regatta.

- Have a daily routine and get out on the course an hour before the start.

CHAPTER 6

The Venue

CHAPTER 6

The Venue

> *"The weather is never normally like this here, you should have been here last week!"*
>
> **– Someone at every regatta or championship I have ever attended.**

Preparation is the secret of all champions, and I am not just referring to the boat.

Logistics

Regatta strategy starts long before the event starts and can start up to a year or more out.

The plan should be to get you, your crew and boat to the event in the best shape possible.

This includes all your equipment, physical fitness and your mental attitude being at peak when the regatta starts.

The earlier that communication and planning gets underway, the less chance you will have arriving with your mind on other matters not associated with racing.

Regatta Housing

At many regatta venues there may be a shortage of adequate or cheap accommodation for you and your supporters.

Championships tend to be held in holiday seasons and the available options are in high demand. Book early and if your plans change you can always cancel.

It is best to be close to town where food and other facilities are available but don't be too far from the sailing venue if at all possible. In many cases the ability to self-cater can be an advantage.

If you are in a holiday destination restaurants can be booked out or not available at times to suit your program.

Another equally important factor is that the type of food that you need may not be catered for by restaurants, so self-catering accommodation and a nearby supermarket may be essential.

Food and Drink

Don't forget race day food and drinks for on the water.

It may make sense to buy all drinks, snacks and basic food items for the whole regatta before racing starts and that way there is no chance that you will find yourself on the water starving or dehydrated.

Transport to and from Accommodation

It's not always practical to have a car. There may be parking constraints at the regatta club or your accommodation may be in a high-density town. So being able to walk or cycle to the venue is a great advantage.

Public transport with a regular timetable is an option but all this needs to be worked out prior to arriving at the regatta.

Location of Support

Yet another great reason to get to a regatta with days in hand is locating an adequate chandlery, sailmaker, rigger and boat builder should urgent repairs be necessary as well as the availability of medical assistance, should that be needed.

Although most organisers have these things listed in their documentation it is still worth checking to make sure each aspect meets your requirements.

Sailing Venue Clubhouse Facilities

Check the club and boat park as soon as you arrive at the regatta town and get a handle on the availability of changing facilities, showers and security for your gear whilst you are on the water.

Are there adequate boat and gear rinsing facilities available?

This is very relevant if you don't have a vehicle to lock your valuables in.

Storage

Is your boat going to be in a secure well-lit area and safe if big winds suddenly hit the site? If not, you may need to make other arrangements.

Launching

Check whether you are launching from the beach or a ramp, and if there is a large fleet and narrow ramp. Make sure that you plan to leave the boat park with plenty of time to get on the course and go through your routine.

Course in Relation to the Boat Park (Course Access)

A couple of days prior to the first race, sail out to the course and note the time it takes to get there.

There is nothing worse than arriving for the first race and not allowing enough time to carry out all your pre-race observations. If that happens you may not be able to adequately plan your race strategy.

Local Knowledge

Arriving at the regatta site early gives you a chance to catch up with the locals and start to get a handle on local knowledge.

It's amazing what can be found out by being out on the track with the them in the days before the regatta, and what can be gleaned by hanging around the club house, boat park and having a few bevvies with local competitors after training.

Weather Patterns

Study the weather history at the venue and forecasts for the time that you will be there in order to have a plan, rather than arriving and then having no time to think through weather strategies.

Geography at the Venue That Could Affect the Wind

When you are out on the course and practising prior to the regatta starting, take note of the land surrounding the course.

Things to notice are cliffs, hills, valleys and peninsulas that will have an effect on the wind when it comes from different directions. You need to look out for the wind bending around the points/headlands – the breeze tends to follow the shape of the land.

As an example, I have seen courses set on enclosed waterways which have had lifts or knocks influenced by roads coming down at right angles to the shoreline.

Look along the shoreline for rivers, creeks and outfalls that may affect you on the course as well.

Tides

Get a copy of the local tide tables, as knowing what the tide is doing at different times whilst you are on the course, will be relevant to tidal flows and currents.

Currents

It's very important to know what the current is doing at the start of the race, as it affects your approach to the line and then where you go on the course and reference to the tide tables will be used in concert with your earlier current observations.

In many instances you can avoid currents by sailing close to shore, where it's shallower and where you may even be able to take advantage of a back eddy. You must factor in tide changes during the race but especially be aware of current when considering laylines.

If you are sailing in a bad current and are sailing toward a part of the course where there is less, sail there as fast as you can even if it means putting the bow down.

On the other hand if you are sailing in a favourable current you can sail higher and a little slower to stay in the current longer.

For some popular regatta venues there are comprehensive current charts, as an example the Solent in the UK or La Rochelle in France.

Calculating Current Across the Course

Even if current charts are available, make an effort to test the current when you arrive at the course. Use something that doesn't float above the surface too much, throw it in next a buoy or some other fixed object and watch its speed and direction.

It is important to do this at various parts of the course, and this should form part of your reconnaissance prior to the regatta.

Underwater Topography

If possible, see if you can get a soundings chart of the course area and surrounding water, this will show you where you should take your current observations, for instance if there is an old river course or underwater canyon across the race track, the water will move more quickly on a flood or ebb tide in that area.

TAKEAWAYS

- Planning a long way out from the regatta will relieve stress and ensure that no important aspect is left to chance.
- Plan to stay within easy commuting or walking distance of the venue.
- A choice of comfortable accommodation ensures a good sleep, which of course assists mindset and sharpness on the course.
- Locate the chandlery, sailmaker and other support services as soon as you get to the venue.
- Arrive at the race venue with days or even weeks to spare in order to practise, get to know the conditions and understand the weather patterns.
- Arriving with time before the event allows you to find all the support services that you may need during the regatta.

CHAPTER 7

Weather, Wind and Clouds

CHAPTER 7

Weather, Wind and Clouds

> "There is no such thing as bad weather, only bad clothes."
>
> — **Old Norwegian Adage**

INTERVIEW

I spoke with Andrew 'Doggy' Palfrey, well known world champion sailor, international coach, gun for hire and all round good bloke, about weather and wind and how he approaches weather planning for each race or regatta.

Q Brett: How do you collect data about weather and wind at a regatta venue especially historical information prior to arriving?

A Andrew: I think the "gold standard" is to try to make contact with a respected local. The main things to speak to them about are:

i.   What are the two or three biggest factors to concern yourself with in terms of racecourse effect (i.e.: Tidal? Geographic features that effect the wind? The characteristics of sea breeze evolution? And so on). You just want to hone in on the big things.

ii. What are the best forecast resources locally? Again, this will save a lot of time. We are so much more fortunate these days in regard to the amount of resource available. The downside can be that there is too much info. You need to hone in on the best resource.

iii. In the lead-up to the event, touch base with this person again and discuss the weather map and what he/she might see as important over coming days.

Q **Brett: Do you put together a plan for the days racing with regard to the forecast?**

A **Andrew:** Yes. First thing would be sail choices, then the sailing kit to take afloat. Sounds simple, but if you are not comfortable, you'll find it harder to get the most from yourself.

Spend the morning continuously checking the sky and water to see if the forecast is playing out – you want to know if the forecast is accurate, in order to gauge the confidence to have in it.

Q **Brett: Obviously, forecasts are general and not necessarily specific to the regatta venue, what notice do you take of the forecast?**

A **Andrew:** Depends on all of the above. If you have done the homework and have done some validation in order to gain confidence, then it can be quite a weapon. If not, well, you'd take it into account, but more likely to sail the fleet and place the boat conservatively.

Q **Brett: How do you call wind shifts and what feedback do you want from your crew?**

A **Andrew:** It's important to get a feel for the range of shifts and what you'd class as mean headings on either tack. This gives you a framework for the decisions during the race.

Regarding feedback, it is critical to know your position relative to the laylines and relative to the fleet.

Q **Brett: Can you tell whether a puff is a lift or a header before it gets to you?**

A **Andrew:** a. I think I have a reasonable eye for that. Not as good as some people I have sailed with!

b. But I think this is a constantly 'improvable' skill. For example, during the pre-race tune-up, I will develop my instincts by looking at an approaching wind line and take a stab at whether it will lift, head or stay the same direction. The resultant change (if any) in the true wind direction will go in the memory bank for later when I see a similar looking wind line approaching.

c. Other things help with this 'instinct'. For example, if we are already on one edge of the wind range, odds are that the next shift will be back towards or beyond the mean.

Q Brett: In an oscillating breeze, how do you work out when to tack?

A Andrew: a. Again, where are we on the course with relation to laylines. I'd be more likely to tack from port to starboard on a 'mean' heading if we only have a few percent left of starboard tack in the leg.

b. Where are we in relation to the fleet? If 90% of the fleet is to our right – and on port tack, you'd be silly to continue on starboard tack for too much longer looking for more left shift. Unless you had established in the pre-race tune-up that gusts are not moving down the course.

c. Where is the true wind direction in relation to what we consider is our 'range' of shift?

Q Brett: Do you take notice of clouds on the course and how do they affect your decision making?

A Andrew: Yes, absolutely. I think broadly speaking, the clouds can tell you a lot about whether the forecast is playing out, or not. This assumes you had that information to hand prior to racing.

Q Brett: What can clouds tell you?

A Andrew: a. Lots…but to highlight a couple of things I look for:

    i. In terms of a sea breeze development, they are fundamental in highlighting the convection above the land

    ii. On a day of squally and rainy conditions, the clouds are your main indicators for where to go and where to avoid going.

   iii.   The approach of a change in conditions be it a tightening of pressure gradient, a front etc.

   b. Basically they are part of the environment in which we make our decisions.

Q **Brett: If the wind shift seems persistent how do you establish a new mean or is this a constant process?**

A **Andrew:** The mean is something we set in our minds, so of course it is quite a fluid number.

Keeping an open mind and constantly updating what is happening and where we are relative to course and laylines is key.

Q **Brett: How do you calculate wind strength in order to set your boat up for the conditions?**

A **Andrew:**   a. I think the keys here are:

   i.   What is the sea-state?

   ii.   How dense does the breeze feel on the sail plan?

   iii.   Are the waves offset to the true wind direction?

   b. I'll try to get a quick feel for these questions in the first couple of minutes in a pre-race line-up. Set the boat up and adjust as necessary using your senses. Then check in with performance relative to other boats and make some simple evaluations based upon your power level and balance.

Q **Brett: If a front is predicted during the race, does your strategy take this in to account?**

A **Andrew:** Yes – you'd be constantly monitoring the sky and the true wind speed and true wind direction.

Q Brett: If you feel a sudden change in temperature either up or down, what can you read in to this?

A Andrew: Tricky one... we all feel when the wind becomes warmer when sailing toward land on a summer's day in an offshore breeze or the colder air filling in when a sea breeze starts to build.

Hard to generalise what this means. Sometimes it is obvious, like the examples here. Other times it can be quite subtle.

I think it is another indicator that things have just changed and you need to be tuned into what it might mean and how it affects your decision-making in the short term.

Q Brett: What effect can a rain squall moving across the course have, and how can you use it to your advantage?

A Andrew: If the squall is generally upwind, I'd be aiming to place the boat near to the leading edge of the rain squall. But not so close that I get engulfed too quickly relative to the fleet.

In general you will find more breeze and shifted direction on the edge. If the rain squall is downwind of the gradient true wind direction, I'd try to get away from it as quickly as I can (or try to avoid it if you are sailing downwind).

In this case the colder air coming from the cloud would generally reduce the true wind speed.

Q Brett: Do you time shifts to get an idea when to expect the next shift, or is it something that you feel?

A Andrew: a. I've never really taken the times of shifts methodically like that

b. I do not write the shift range down.

c. I seem to have a good recall for the numbers

Q Brett – Where is the best place to get your weather information from?

A **Andrew:** I have developed a trust for PredictWind. Very user-friendly. Gives a good over-view snapshot, but allows you to dig deeper into the bigger picture synoptic and cloud situation with a few clicks. I like it.

Q Brett: Do you look at a weather map and what do you read from it?

A **Andrew:** Yes – I think it important for sailors to know what is driving the weather and what are the two or three biggest influencing factors. This helps over the course of an event.

I just like to know what is driving the wind we see and how might that change over the course of the day or the event. I think it is just another component in developing your decision-making instincts.

FROM OTHER SOURCES

Clouds

There are 4 categories of clouds:

1. High clouds, 16,000–43,000 feet – cirrus, cirrostratus and cirrocumulus.

   Cirrus clouds indicate fair weather in the immediate future but they can also indicate a change in weather within the next 24 hours.

   Cirrus clouds tell the arrival of a warm front associated with low pressure but can also precede a cold front.

   If you watch the direction that the streaks are pointing it gives you an idea of which way the weather front is moving.

   Cirrus clouds don't have an immediate effect on surface wind direction and speed and are generally situated a long way from a front.

2. Middle clouds, 6,500–23,000 feet – altostratus and altocumulus.

   Altostratus are grey and/or blue clouds and indicate a storm in the near future and normally precede rain.

   Altocumulus are greyish-white and if they are present in the morning you can expect thunderstorms in the afternoon.

3. Low clouds – below 6,500 feet – stratus, stratocumulus and nimbostratus.

   Stratus are placed just above the ground and regularly bring drizzle.

   Stratocumulus don't bring rain and tend to cover the whole sky and generally come in rows or and patches.

4. Clouds with vertical growth – below 6500 feet to 40,000 feet plus – cumulus and cumulonimbus.

   Cumulus clouds are commonly referred to as 'cotton ball' and are associated with fair weather but beware of any vertical growth because this signals the start of a large storm.

   Cumulonimbus clouds are cumulus clouds that have grown to an anvil shape and the anvil tends to point in the direction of the storm and bring rain, lightning and hail.

   The cloud can appear as though it is boiling and this means the cloud is actively growing, with warm moist air rising, eventually cool air will start to come down which creates gusts.

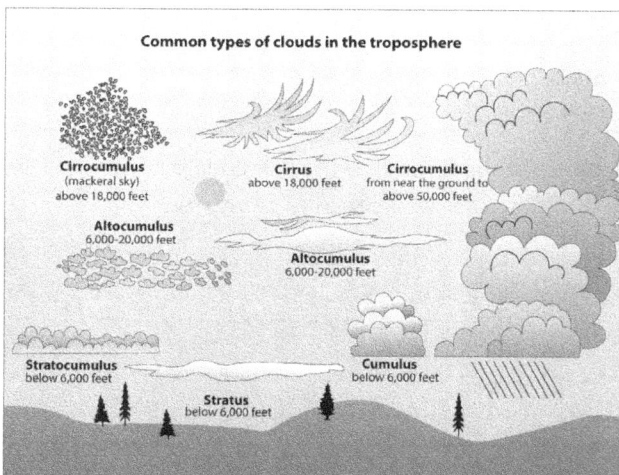

Common types of clouds in the troposphere

Cirrocumulus (mackeral sky) above 18,000 feet

Cirrus above 18,000 feet

Cirrocumulus from near the ground to above 50,000 feet

Altocumulus 6,000-20,000 feet

Altocumulus 6,000-20,000 feet

Stratocumulus below 6,000 feet

Cumulus below 6,000 feet

Stratus below 6,000 feet

How the Weather Works and the Causes of Wind.

Water covers 70% of Earth's surface and the atmosphere envelopes all of it. This layer of gases is subject to influence from terrestrial and extra-terrestrial forces.

Earth's atmosphere, gravity, sunlight, oceans and topography all dictate certain cycles of air movement. A number of these cycles affect each other causing clouds to form.

Wind is the movement of air molecules from one location to another and is caused by differences in atmospheric pressure on our rotating planet. Air will also be deflected by the Coriolis Effect which means that the airflow is not direct.

Sea breezes – During the day, the land is heated up by the sun and the surrounding air absorbs the heat. The heated air rises which creates a low pressure area at ground level.

Because the sea heats more slowly than the land, the air above the sea is cooler and this air moves in over the land to fill the low pressure area created by the heated rising air.

The sea breeze is much more prominent in summer and spring when the differences of temperature and thus air pressure are greater.

True and Apparent Wind

True wind is wind that is not affected by the movement of the observer.

Apparent wind is the wind felt by an observer who is moving and is the relative velocity of the wind in relation to the observer.

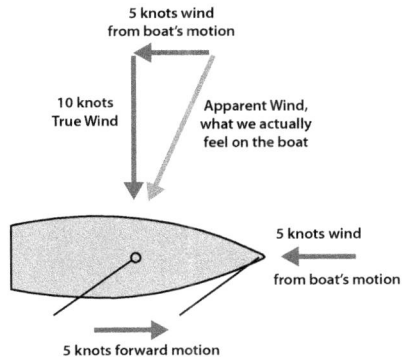

5 knots wind
from boat's motion

10 knots
True Wind

Apparent Wind,
what we actually
feel on the boat

5 knots wind
from boat's motion

5 knots forward motion

TRUE and APPARENT WIND

Wind Shear

Wind shear is a change in true wind direction with altitude, and wind gradient is a change in true wind speed with altitude. When combined, they affect the wind seen by your sail at different heights, and may considerably affect how you trim your sail on each tack.

Wind shear is caused by the relative difference of the air and water temperature and friction at the water's surface. Wind direction and speed at the top of your mast can vary considerably from that experienced at deck level, and your sails must be trimmed accordingly. This is more relevant the larger the boat with a taller mast and not as relevant in a dinghy.

Telltales are useful in setting your sail to deal with wind shear and you may also feel boat speed or helm differences on each tack, which will mean you must adjust your sails to suit.

Wind shear is a clue of a wind shift to come and it's a good bet that if the wind is sheared to the right up top, you will see a shift to the right at the surface at a later stage.

Puffs and Lulls

- A puff is an increase in breeze and can take the form of a directional puff or fan puff. The initial puff is a fan puff – it is obvious and spreads out from its source.

- The remnants are a directional puff and the crew needs to let the helmsman know how long before it will hit and the intensity. An out loud countdown is a good way to pass the information on.

- Lulls appear before and after puffs and the caller should let the helmsman know when they are coming so that adjustments can be made to the rig and settings.

Reading a Weather Map

- The lines on a weather map are called isobars and wind blows almost exactly along the isobars and arrows will show you the direction.

- The closer the isobars, the stronger the wind, though this does vary with latitude.

- Because of the spin out effect wind can be 20% higher out of a high and up to 20% lighter in to a low.

- Surface wind leaks across the isobars towards low pressure.

- Isobars are only smoothed out approximations and only give you general wind flow.

A low pressure is a funnel of wind spiralling inwards and forcing warm air upwards, and a high's centre has high pressure and light winds, with winds pushing outwards and stronger winds at its extremities.

Thermal and Sea Breezes

Sea breezes are caused by unequal heating and cooling of adjacent land and sea surfaces. A sea breeze blows from the sea to the land and is caused by the differential heating.

The warmed air rises over the land and cool air from over the sea is drawn inland. The ascending air returns seaward in what is known as the upper return current (see the diagram below).

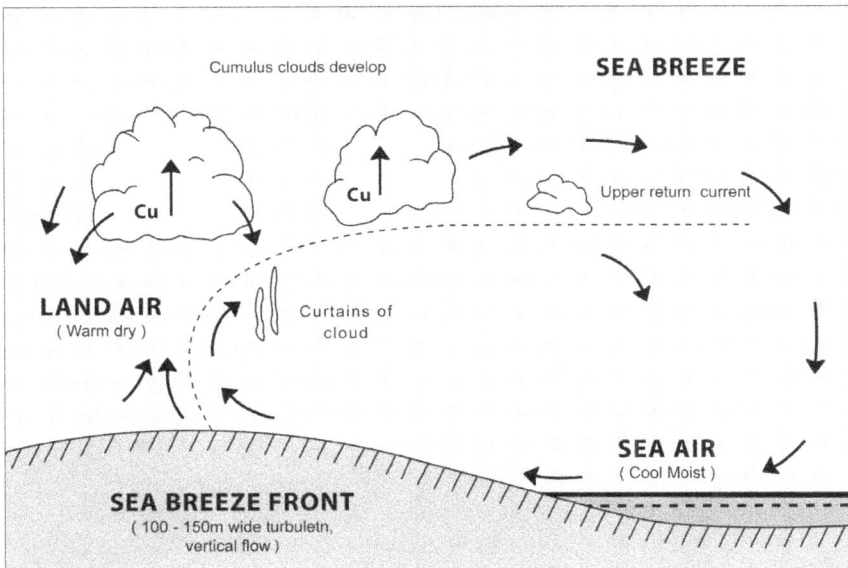

How to Distinguish Oscillating and Persistent Shifts

If boats make gains on both the left- and right-hand side of the course it is a fair indication that you have an oscillating breeze.

On the other hand, if one side of the course is always favoured it is more than likely that you have a persistent shift.

A sea breeze generally shifts persistently as it builds and then shifts slowly back as it weakens later in the day.

It pays to watch other boats especially in the early part of each beat to determine the type of shifts on the course.

TAKEAWAYS

- Make contact with a respected local when researching expected wind patterns at a regatta venue.
- It is as important to select the right clothing for the day as selecting the right sails.
- Get out on the course early and get a feel for the range of shifts and establish your mean headings on either tack.
- Crew feedback on wind shifts must take in to account the laylines and how you are relative to the fleet.
- Clouds give you an indication as to whether the forecast is playing out as predicted.
- 'Predictwind' is one of the more user friendly sources of weather information.
- If boats make gains on each side of the course it is an indication that the breeze is oscillating.
- If one side of the course is favoured the shift is likely to be persistent.
- A sea breeze generally shifts persistently and shifts slowly back at the end of the day as it weakens.

CHAPTER 8

Championship and Regatta Strategy

CHAPTER 8

Championship and Regatta Strategy

> *"My goal in sailing isn't to be brilliant or flashy in individual races, just to be consistent over the long run."*
>
> **– Dennis Conner (USA) four-time winning America's cup skipper.**

INTERVIEW

I spoke with Glenn Bourke to give us some insight in to championship and regatta strategy. Glenn is currently the CEO of the wildly successful Hamilton Island which is home of Hamilton Island race week.

Not only is Glenn a successful businessman but he is a high achieving competitive sailor with multiple Olympic, World and National championship successes to his name.

Q Brett: Do you approach a regatta differently in big or small fleets?

A Glenn: A little bit. I guess I've predominately done most of my sailing career in big fleets. And I certainly have a system that I employ in big fleets, and some of it's applicable to small fleets, and some it's not so applicable.

For example, before technology in boats, I used to start maybe a third or a quarter down from the favoured end of the line, or a quarter up from the favoured end of the line if it was for pin.

The reason for that was that usually there's a bulge at the top end of the line or the bottom end of the line, if it's favoured quite a bit.

You can generally get yourself clear air and away off the line and not be seen by the committee boat if you start a little bit away from that mad pack that generally goes over the line early.

So you might call it a conservative start, it's probably not the Hail Mary start, but it's one whereby you tuck yourself away and if the whole fleet goes, you're probably not seen from an OCS or maybe you're not an OCS because you're behind the line, but they're bulged out underneath you.

You're still clear and going, but you're not in the ruckus of the chaos at the end of the big fleet.

In smaller fleets, I think you can have the opportunity to be a bit more aggressive and to take the favoured end of the line because there's not as much carnage there, and you can pre-manoeuvre and do whatever else you need to do.

Some of it depends on who is your main competition, if it's a small fleet and everybody's even, then you want to get the best start. You want to get into the first shift first.

If it's a small fleet, and there's one other competitor that's tough, you want to make sure that you get a slightly better start than that person so that you can control them up the first beat and take advantage of getting off the line a little bit better.

Brett: And so talk about big fleets. What are some big fleet basic strategies? If you're sailing in a regatta, obviously, it's going to be a number of races. Do you use a big fleet strategy?

Glenn: There's a number of them. First of all, you've got to be fast. In a big fleet, if you want to get to the front end of the fleet, you have to be fast.

If you can jump out of the start and clear yourself, tack across a group of boats and get into a really clear position, you ought to take that opportunity and do it straight away.

It depends where you end up at the first mark as to what your strategy might be after that.

You can't compete in a big fleet unless you're fast because you're going to get spat out, and then you are just going to be looking for crumbs on the table rather than being assertive in your strategy or where you're putting the boat compared to the fleet.

It also changes from the beginning of the regatta to the end of the regatta.

At the end of the regatta, you've got to be more perfect. At the end of the regatta, you've got to watch your opposition.

You make a transitional strategy from being very fast, off the line well, getting to the first shift and trying to get around the top mark in good order.

In the beginning of the regatta you are watching where your competitors are, being generally in the right place, being generally a bit more conservative and to cover their moves rather than necessarily trying to get the perfect regatta, or the perfect race under your belt.

Q **Brett: I'm assuming that when you go to an event, you develop a plan?**

A **Glenn:** Well you have your aspiration in the beginning so you know what you want to achieve, and you're trying to learn about the venue and understand what you think the idiosyncrasies of that venue are, so you're capable of making changes as you need them.

The plan will change based on the input that you get. I think sailing strategy is very much like playing chess. What's the other guy, done relative to what you've done?

Can you factor that in, in a quick way and be adaptable enough to alter the destiny of a race or a leg, or the regatta itself?

So, it's always moving pawns and knights to set yourself up relative to the competition. I think it's an actuarial kind of composition. I'm always thinking about the numbers in the event. Where am I?

If I'm thirtieth at the top mark and I really need to get into the top ten again, I'm going to be a bit more aggressive at the bottom such that I've got to get myself clear, I've got to get to the favoured side of the course. I've got to take a little bit more a risk to try and get myself up to tenth because I know that counting a thirtieth is going to hurt me.

If I'm first around the top mark, I know that I'm going to leg it on port tack from out of the bottom mark, and then cover the fleet and try and make people do what you want them to do to shut the race down, to get the least reaction out of the fleet.

If there's one guy that's inconsequential to the event, that's taking a flier out to the left, I'm going to let him go and just hope that my plan's better than his.

Q Brett: How do you plan to approach the layline if there's a big fleet and you're back ten, fifteenth or something like that? Obviously that's going to be pretty critical. What is your thinking there?

Glenn: Again, you got to be adaptable. If you're coming in and you're under the lay-line, and there's a big raft up, if somebody crosses in front of you or just behind you and opens a track up, and you need to get out to that starboard hand layline, because ultimately the only defence you have is being on the starboard hand layline, you got to be out there and in clear air.

So if a guy ducks you and he's creating a hole for you, tack on his hip, take a dig out, get to the layline, and come back again.

Don't get trapped at the top mark doing a series of donuts trying to find a hole of all the starboard tackers that are coming in there.

Don't get caught late, be pre-emptive. Make your decisions early.

Know that the only safe place to be is on the starboard layline, and usually with clear air. And understand that if you're really deep, they're going to rack up further and further and further outside the starboard hand layline.

There's just occasionally an opportunity if you're in thirtieth place to stay to the left and then find a hole coming back in.

Usually, if you're in the top 20 boats, and you're coming into the top mark, you better not be that guy that gets trapped out of the top mark because you see it happen so often. They tack, they don't give them room.

They've got to run behind 15 boats before they can find a hole to tack into, and they've got to come all the way back again. So yeah, you've really got to be pre-thinking it as much as you can and take your opportunity to get out to the right at the end.

Q **Brett:** Coming up to that weather mark, or a leeward mark for that matter, how far out do you plan the next leg?

A **Glenn:** My first thing is get yourself clear. Get yourself on the favoured side. Look for where the pressure is coming from. Try to be on that side of it compared to the other guys in the fleet. Understand what you're trying to do.

As you're halfway down the leg, it'll depend on whether it's a very homogenous breeze day, where it's just oscillating nicely or whether it's shifting back and forward, and there's puff or whatever.

If it's a day where there's lots of change, lots of shifts happening, lots of gusts happening, you probably don't want to make your decision until you're right down near the bottom somewhere.

If there's a gate at the bottom, am I going to go left or am I going to go right? Which way is the pressure and which way is headed on the run, so which side is the lifted side on the next beat?

If it's a homogenous day, you sort of know where the oscillations are. You know where you are in the fleet. If you're behind, you're looking for an opportunity so you might go to a different mark to the guys in front of you just to get clear air and get back in the race.

You might follow them because it's so biased to one side that you just have to do that anyway. But you might have decided halfway down the run that the favoured side is the right or the left.

My predominant reaction is to go that way even if I've got to follow guys, get myself clear, tack off, get clear air, come back again, and stay to the right, those things evolve as you're going down the run.

You need to be thinking about it all the time. You can't go and lock in and say, "I'm definitely going to the right hand side," if the factors that are affecting you are changing over time.

So stay alert, stay adaptable, have a general plan, and then refine it as you get towards the bottom mark would be my advice.

Q **Brett: There are times to take risks and there are times to be conservative. Obviously it depends on what's at stake, doesn't it?**

A Glenn: You know the guys in the fleet who are the risk takers. They usually don't win the regatta.

They're usually starting at the pin, banging out to the left, and getting trapped out by, a hundred boats that cross their bow and tack on top of them on the way back to the top mark.

They'll win two races in the series, and they'll come eighth in the regatta. They got heaps of pace, and they're far too dramatic for sail boat racing and winning regattas. And that's just the function of their nature. Most of them can't change themselves.

To be at the top end of the fleet consistently, you have to be able to be conservative generally, but adapt whenever opportunities or issues arise for you.

Q **Brett – Are there times when it's more prudent to stay with the fleet and sail with the fleet rather than go off on your own?**

A Glenn: When you're constructing a regatta win, it's safer to stay with the fleet and I would much prefer to have a third with no risk than a first with medium amount of risk.

If I'm constructing a regatta, I'm trying to get on the podium every day. Can I get a decent result every day? And I know that the more I hang it out there and do dramatic things, the greater the risk.

If the fleet splits in two, and half go left and half go right, you've got to take a punt on which side do you think is correct. If the fleet is predominately going right, and three guys go left, don't worry about the left guys.

Stay with the fleet because at worst, you're going to get into fourth place, and you can count that and your main players are on your side of the course.

It's an accounting function where you just trying to work out risk versus reward. If you're fast, there's even more reason to stay with the fleet.

I know that Tom Slingsby in his day, was a fast Laser sailor, he would know when to just stick with them because he was going to make small gains if he stuck with them.

He might have had the opportunity of a huge gain when he went a different way, but why do that when you can stick with them and beat them anyway?

Q **Brett: What's the one thing that a sailor who is looking to improve should concentrate on or one thing that they should get better at to improve, to drag themselves up the Leader Board?**

A **Glenn:** The thing that you need to do in sailboat racing is focus on the most important thing at that time. So when it's getting off the starting line, it's creating a hole for yourself and jumping at the gun, and going.

The next thing is to clear yourself as you're going up the beat.

The thing after that is to work out how to get to the starboard layline so that you're clear and coming into the top mark.

The thing after that is, where is the breeze shifting downwind? Where is the pressure geographically on this course?

Quite often, we get carried away with whether the main sheets got a knot in it, or whether my quads are hurting because I'm hiking so hard, or whether the boom vang or the sail depth is not absolutely correct.

What I would say to everybody is try and focus on the most important thing.

I have this friend of mine, and she said to me once, "The most important thing is to keep the most important thing the most important thing." And I thought it was beautiful in the context of sailing because we can so often get preoccupied with not the most important thing when we're sailing.

So if I had any advice, it would be try to concentrate. Try and think about what's the thing of the paramount importance right now.

The other thing is, is you'll never go fast if you've got crappy gear. You'll never be able to compete if you've got crappy gear. So don't train with worn out horrible gear because you'll learn bad habits.

Make sure that your boats well prepared and that you're comfortable in it, and it suits you and how you sail, and spend a bit of time preparing.

FROM OTHER SOURCES

Go for the Shift or the Pressure?

Don't chase shifts, it can be tempting, when you see a boat nearby on a huge lift, to sail toward that shift, however, this rarely works. More often than not, you sail on a header to reach the other boat and by the time you get there, generally the shift is gone.

You are better off focusing on sailing in the wind you have. Use other boats as a guide to know how much you are lifted or headed, but don't try to sail for their shift.

It's a better option to go out of your way for better pressure, especially in lighter air

The Compass or the Fleet?

It's easy to get mesmerised by the compass and what it tells us but having said that it's still an important tool to refer to during a race.

We have reference marks for everything on our boats, sheets, board angle, jib cars and so on and the compass can be used as a reference to how we are doing against the fleet.

Sometimes merely looking at the boats in the fleet that you are racing will give you a better indication of whether you are being lifted or headed than the compass alone.

When and How to Cut Your Losses

A boat well to weather of you and slightly back on your hip experiences a favourable wind shift, what do you do?

If you don't get the same lift you should tack. Relative to you opponents course you are lifted and you are sailing towards the new breeze.

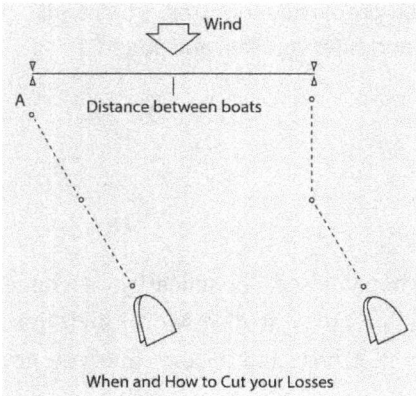

When and How to Cut your Losses

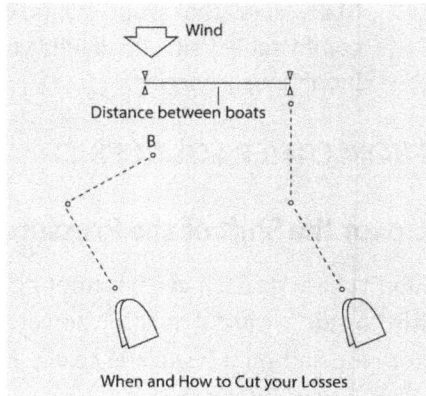

When and How to Cut your Losses

Don't Let Greed Ruin Your Race

Staying on a lift when going upwind when you can see that the fleet is sailing towards a higher pressure band will mean that you will eventually lose out even though you may have been sailing a higher angle.

The fleet will get to the higher pressure fist and will sail faster and if the pressure is a knock, they will be able to tack in the new breeze thus putting distance on you regardless of your higher angle.

Cross the pack when you can and take the advantage when you get it, don't be greedy.

TAKEAWAYS

- In a big fleet you have to be fast and can't rely on tactics alone.
- Develop a plan for a regatta and part of this involves learning the idiosyncrasies of the venue.
- Always be adaptable when approaching the layline, be pre-emptive and make your decisions early.
- Plan your next leg early but be thinking about it all the time, stay alert and be adaptable.
- Risk takers rarely win regattas.
- To be at the top end of the fleet you generally need to be conservative.
- When racing you need to think about the most important thing at that time. Concentrate on the thing that is of paramount importance right now.
- You will never go fast with crappy gear, don't train with horrible gear as you will only learn bad habits.
- Use the headings of boats in the fleet as a guide in conjunction with the compass readings.

CHAPTER 9

The Start

CHAPTER 9

The Start

> *"If you get a bad start you must still go the way that is the fastest, you should not get flustered and start taking chances or going off on a flyer, never do the opposite of what the leading boats are doing"*
>
> **Paul Elvstrom (Danish) Four Olympic golds, 11 world titles in eight different classes.**

INTERVIEW

I asked two time 505 world champion and twice runner up Mike Holt a couple of questions about starting, to see if I could grasp some of the things that made him a champion.

Q Brett: Describe your overall start strategy.

A Mike: For me, whether it is a line or gate start, I am focused on ensuring having a runway to leeward and being at full speed when I start.

I then want to be able to climb when I can and foot when I need to get to the next shift in good shape and aiming to control my destiny.

Q Brett: How do you keep your lane off the start line?

A Mike: The key to this is in making sure you can get to full speed at or before the start.

Once racing in a crowded area you have to keep moving between height and speed, too much of one over the other will get you in trouble.

Height, height, speed. Repeat until the space around you is acceptable to sail your own race.

Q **Brett: If you get baulked or get an ordinary start, what do you do to recover?**

A **Mike:** Important to recognise this quickly and then stop the bleeding. Tack, take sterns and look at your options.

Unless you are utterly convinced that left is the way to go, in that case, suck it up and sail fast, better to go slow the right way than fast the wrong way.

Q **Brett: What is the crew's role in the start sequence?**

A **Mike:** Feed information and make sure the boat can still move. Talk about time, where there are gaps, who may invade your space and attempting to work out time on distance to the start.

Q **Brett: What are you trying to accomplish at the start?**

A **Mike:** Generally what I am trying to do is put myself in the right place to execute my 'plan' for the first beat, so if I want to go one side or the other, make sure I can get there.

Q **Brett: Do you have a favourite way to approach each start?**

A **Mike:** It varies between a line start and a gate start. For a line I like a late port tack approach to where I want to start, especially effective if I want the 'left' end of the line.

If it is a gate start we are monitoring the wind continually, picking up the trends as best we can. Same goals, set ourselves up to be going the way we have discussed.

We will then look for the best space in the area we want to be starting in and then apply subtle pressure on the windward boat to give us space to sail fast off of the line.

Q **Brett: How important is it to maintain consistency in your starting approach?**

A **Mike:** I think a plan is important, but adapting is also important.

New facts that appear, a wind shift, too many boats where you are can all require a rethink and we will adapt quickly when we have to.

BUT you must discuss clearly, the what and why between helm and crew.

Q Brett: What are the most important tactical skills for starting?

A Mike: You must be confident that your speed is competitive and you know what the first move you are planning is.

If all goes well, you can execute on it, however, if it doesn't, make sure you 'stem the bleeding' as fast as you can and start looking for opportunities.

Q Brett: What can you do to become a better starter?

A Mike: Practise! Work out a plan and execute.

Q Brett: Is there a routine you follow when getting ready for a start?

A Mike: We tend to have a standard approach to every race. Sail as much of the first beat as time will allow.

Get our compass numbers dialled and agree what the averages are.

Check tide, course, bearing to first mark etc.

Discuss what we each think and if there is consensus, lock in the plan. If we are not aligned we discuss why we are thinking differently and agree a plan.

We will then drink some water and keep checking our numbers.

We will not go into "final approach" until the last 60 seconds. Quick check that we are still good with our plan. Leverage the best hole we can and then, off!

Q Brett: Do you spend time tuning up with other boats prior to the start?

A Mike: Absolutely, vital to make sure you are set up where you need to be and fully up to speed.

Good to have a partner that you do this with so that you have a known check on this.

Q **Brett: What do you do when, after tuning up and just prior to the start, you find you speed is average or worse?**

A **Mike:** Panic!! You have to make sure first, everything is where it should be, did the ram get un-cleated, is the rake wrong etc. Assuming all this is ok, board, vang, sheet loads.

Are you high and slow, low etc., and adjust and re-line up with your partner again.

Have you improved? Keep working until it feels right.

Q **Brett: When you are looking upwind at the course, what are the keys to reading the wind on the water?**

A **Mike:** Looking generally for more wind, what the geography looks like, where the wind shifts may be.

So is the wind coming off the shore or is it a clean fetch?

Do we see more white horses on one side or the other? Be careful though as sun and shade can confuse.

We are also looking at clouds, where are they going. Generally I would sail towards the clouds.

Q **Brett: If you get on the course later than you would like, what do you concentrate on?**

A **Mike:** Set the alarm for earlier the next day!!! You really cannot afford to be late to the race track, it puts you behind the curve.

But when it does happen, focus on the quick wins, dial in the wind direction, make sure that the boat is on the right settings for the conditions and hopefully you can wing it on what way to go.

Very important now to communicate between helm and crew. Are we ok for speed, need more height, eyes out of the boat checking everything out and reporting back to each other.

I also spoke with Sam Haines, who had just come back from the 2016 Etchells World Championship regarding their starting routine.

Q Brett: Once you're on the water and before the start, what do you do as part of your preparation?

A Sam: You want to be at the starting area an hour prior to a race. We would have a sandwich on the way out to the start line and get comfortable put the gear on that we are going to race in, then do a little upwind exercise.

Hopefully, with a mate that you have an understanding with, to do a little two boat up wind preparation, probably for 15 minutes then pull the kite up, come downwind.

You need to be really intense as if you were racing, pumping the kite and throwing in a few gybes.

Get back to the starting area, by then you're probably looking at a half an hour, 20 minutes prior to the start.

We have another mini-break have a water and a sandwich.

By that time the committee will have your start line in. Then we would sail up wind from the middle of the line again, put in couple of tacks, and get your numbers.

You're getting within ten minutes of the five-minute gun at this time. Then you've got an understanding of whether it's a left or right lane.

What we do at that point is sail to whichever end we're think is the correct one to start at. This is all about having your head switched on and that we are actually racing. We're not cruising up and down behind the line.

What you'll find in any big fleet is everyone reaches up and down behind the line flogging their gear and no one's really switched on.

You are actually intensely getting into your racing, you've done this little bit of homework so you know when you do a head to wind with two and a half minutes to go and the breeze is actually gone right that you actually need to get up towards the boat, you're actually in that mode.

Whereas if you've just sailed up and down you don't actually know where the wind is.

FROM OTHER SOURCES

Favoured End (line starts)

To select the favoured end of the line, go head to wind to see which end you are pointing towards– this will be the favoured end.

Another method to establish the favoured end is to simply sail along the line, tack and sail back and see where your sails are set, if you are over-sheeted on one tack you are going more upwind, so the end of the line that you are pointing at is the favoured end to start.

If you have a compass you simply compare the angle of the line with the angle of the wind.

Remember to factor in the wind shifts that you have made a note of when sailing the first leg prior to the start. It is your aim to get to the first shift first.

Where to Start

The longer and more biased the line the more important it is to start closer to the favoured end.

Once you have decided which end is the favoured, hang around the middle of the line so as not to give away your intentions.

If the line is heavily biased, you need to start as close to that end as possible and if you intend to port tack the fleet don't hang around the pin as this too signals your intentions.

Current

The pre-race observations you made by being on the course early need to take account of any current and you must factor this in to your start.

OCS

No matter how good a starter you are you will occasionally find yourself over early and you need to think about recovery. It pays to know the rules for restarting.

Keep a sharp eye on the start boat for flags and if you consider you may have been over, have a plan to get back and restart.

If you do return to clear the line, keeping a clear head – knowing which side of the course is best could mean that you are not hurt too badly.

Nothing is worse than sailing a whole race only to find that your score did not count.

Course to the Windward Mark

In an ideal world, the course to the windward mark is directly upwind from the starting line.

Unfortunately the course to the first mark is rarely perfect so visually locating the mark is essential for planning your start and upwind tactics.

As a rule, if the mark is off to one side you should plan to sail the long tack first. Other things that you must factor in though are wind shifts, as noted in your pre-race time on the course, the side of the course with better pressure, obstacles such as peninsulas, hills and of course current.

Knowing Your Rights

The same rules that apply in open water situations, apply at the start.

Rule 14 requires boats, at all times, to "avoid contact with another boat if reasonably possible, also, if your crew fends off to avoid damage, and remember, if your crew touches the other boat's hull, it's contact.

If you push an offending boat backward and push your own boat forward, fending off in this manner breaks Rule 42.1, propulsion, and probably Rule 2, fair sailing, as well.

Holding Your Position

One obvious way to slow the boat is to luff the sails. Don't turn the bow into the wind, just dump your sheets for a full luff.

An alternative to luffing is over-trimming. When reaching, trimming the sails to close-hauled will slow the boat, it's much quicker to over-trim then ease (or head up).

Oversteering is an effective way to kill time, sweeping turns increase your sailing distance and slow the boat, and sharp turns can slow the boat dramatically.

The double tack is another great time-waster – a double tack scrubs off a lot of speed and shifts you to the right on the line. A bonus is you are able to bear off and accelerate at the appropriate time.

The First Hundred Metres

The first few minutes of a race, between the start and the first shift, determines where the boats will be when the first crucial shift occurs and who will gain relative to the boats you are racing.

Big gains or losses are made at that moment, and on a short leg those gains may persist for the remainder of that leg.

Even if another shift occurs, there will be little time for the advantaged boats to consolidate their gains, therefore the boat that gains the most in the first shift is typically the boat to get to the weather mark first.

Getting Clear in Big Fleets

When you have an ordinary start due to either being in the second row or another boat closing the gap that you had established, get clear of other boats as quickly as you can and head toward clear air in order to stay in the hunt.

Tack on to port if need be, interestingly there is a twist in the breeze as it heads through the fleet giving those on port tack a lift as they cross behind.

Of course you are searching for clear air, but if the left is favoured tack back as soon as you can.

A starboard tack behind the fleet in dirty air is much more painful than port.

If you are having more bad starts than good consider starting closer to the right hand end of the line, from this position you are closer to the clear air.

Now this sounds great, and why wouldn't you always start here? In the case of a gate start those that start well and early, especially if the wind is not moving drastically all over the place, will get to the shifts first.

The favoured end of the starting line may be the best place to start most of the time, but when it's shifty, ignore the opposite end at your peril.

On a leg where you expect frequent shifts, you need to start on the lifted tack, tack when headed beyond the median wind direction, and sail another lifted tack until you reach another header.

If you start on starboard and you know it is down, tack on to port as soon as you can get clear air.

TAKEAWAYS

- Get out to the course area at least an hour before the start to get your head in the boat and set up for the conditions.

- During your pre-race sailing check the current to see how it correlates with your pre-regatta research.

- Before the start, tune up with someone you know is quick in the conditions.

- At a gate or line start make sure you always have a runway to leeward and you are at full speed when the gun goes.

- If you get a bad start, tack immediately when able or do something to stop the bleeding.

- Communication between crew members is essential, feedback the helmsman requires is about gaps, who may drop in on you, and how far you are back from the line.

- After your upwind fact gathering session prior to the start keep an eye upwind for changes indicated by whitecaps, boats up the course plus cloud movement and development.

- A starboard tack behind the fleet in dirty air is way more damaging than port tacking the fleet.

CHAPTER 10

Upwind

CHAPTER 10

Upwind

> **Skipper** to crew(who is about five feet farther forward)
> "Are we going to cross?"
> **Crew** to skipper "Well, I am".

INTERVIEW

To get a better understanding of upwind considerations I interviewed multitalented and high-achieving dinghy and one-design sailor Noel Drennan.

Q Brett: How do you recognise whether a shift is velocity-driven or an actual shift?

A Noel: Essentially, most shifts will usually happen with a velocity drop or a velocity increase, so before the start of the race I try and get my head to wind reading and check the wind. I'll try to do it in the lulls or in a gust and see if there's a pattern there, and go from there.

Q Brett: What's the most important trim adjustment when you're going upwind with the velocity up and down?

A Noel: I think, just as simple as it is, it's the main sheet. It does so much in all boats, dinghies to keel boats.

The main sheet is the absolute key adjustment for the balance and trim.

Q Brett: I think you are the main sheet trimmer on the Alinghi RC 44?

A Noel: Most of the boats I sail on, I've been somewhat pigeonholed into a main sheet trimmer position, essentially I guess because I do a lot of steering.

It's quite often that if you're steering and you don't have a very good main sheet trimmer, the work with the balance of the boat more so than just the trim of the sail is key. For me that's the difference between the better main sheet trimmers and headsail trimmers.

Main sheet trimmers essentially trim the boat to the overall balance more so than just looking at the mainsail and "it looks good today."

Q **Brett: One of the things I've noticed with some keel boat guys is that they don't feel... they feel after it happens, that they reactive rather than proactive, whereas you feel it coming.**

A **Noel:** I think that's been a very important factor for my success that I have the dinghy feel. But I've sailed a lot on keel boats, so you're feeling what's happening with the boat, it's loading up or unloading or the mainsheet's too tight for acceleration, whatever it is.

On a keel boat you'll have your instruments package that will quantify that, but if you have the feel from previous dinghy sailing you will be ahead of the instruments and that's what you need to be.

Q **Brett: Mat Belcher was saying that he quite often trains with a Velocitec if they're training on their own, which I found interesting. A guy at his level... what do you think of that?**

A **Noel:** We do that quite a bit even in Etchells, just for two boat testing or even though they are not allowed by the rules, you can put them on in your practise racing, then it's pretty good.

Q **Brett: As you approach the weather mark and you get lifted ten degrees above the mark, how would you handle this?**

A **Noel:** In an Etchells its tough, because if you're back a bit, you're going to be overlaid anyway, so I guess I would probably sail above the mark to take the shift and get above just for the clean lane around the mark.

Somebody will gain by putting the bow down and going at the mark, but in an Etchells if a port tacker comes in and just hits you, and then two tacks, it's a big loss.

Q Brett: You hear often that you should always sail towards the next shift. Is there a reason why you should sail towards the next shift?

A Noel: Not really, but it does work out usually as an advantage. It really depends if it's more likely to be a header on one side of the course or not, but I don't think it's always a golden rule that you should sail towards the next shift, because it might be a lift and you might end up being to leeward of everybody.

Q Brett: How do clouds influence your upwind strategy?

A Noel: They are a pretty big part of it. I'll always look up and look at the clouds, so if I was sailing in Melbourne, for sure I'd be looking for:

1. The sea breeze clouds building on the land, or

2. If it's any sort of southerly or westerly, just the cloud formations out to sea, because you'd better be going upwind to them.

I've done a reasonable amount of ocean racing, and in the Volvo ocean race you sail with really good navigators and when they come up on deck and tell you "look at the cloud, go to the right-hand side of it and you'll be lifted, or stay away from that one".

You learn what to stay away from or if it's safe to go towards it, which side of the clouds you're going to be lifted and which side you're going to be headed, so I think it's a pretty important thing to do.

Q Brett: Obviously you look at which way the clouds are traveling, but do the type of clouds make a difference?

A Noel: The type of clouds and also – it's very easy these days – go on the website and find out what the actual gradient of the upper-level winds are and it's more often than not the wind usually shifts towards the upper gradient winds, so it's not actually hard to find out about most venues.

Q **Brett: When you're looking up the course, what goes through your mind and what do you look for?**

A **Noel:** I'll usually just simply analyse by eye or look at the clouds and obviously the formation of the clouds because there's likely to be less wind under the cloud, but essentially by eye.

Just by looking at the water, I look for changes or other visual clues such as changes in texture of the water, for whitecaps, or just visual change, and I think half the time you get a pretty good feel for what the pressure is and where the lulls are – essentially by eye.

Q **Brett: If you're steering, you've got to concentrate on what you're doing, do you have a particular person you nominate to keep their eye up the course?**

A **Noel:** I'll usually have one of my crew looking at the extremities of the course and I like them to look and say, "I think there's more wind to the right or less" and just give me the information so then I can turn around and have a quick snapshot every couple of minutes.

I actually think it's a good thing if you don't look at it all the time, because when you have little snapshots and you've been given the right information, it's a pretty good way of getting a solid feel for what's going to happen wind-wise.

Q **Brett: You often hear it said that you've got to sail the long tack first, why is that?**

A **Noel:** I think it's a pretty good rule unless you really know what's going to happen next.

That's something about bigger boats that's helped me in smaller boats because it's all essentially getting down to numbers.

You just get a good picture of why you want to sail the long tack, essentially because you don't really know what's going to happen next.

When you're getting close to the top mark you don't want to end up on one layline, you just essentially want to have options.

Q **Brett: Should you sail for puffs or shifts?**

A Noel: Essentially it's the little bit to do with the boat. If it's a boat like in an Etchells, if you're racing in six to eight knots, its windspeed.

Over probably ten, it's probably shift.

Downwind in a planing boat I go for windspeed every time.

Q **Brett: When you're going upwind, what sort of feedback are you looking for from your crew? Do you talk about it beforehand and say, "this is what I want you to say"?**

A Noel: It's predetermined roles, so there's no point in an Etchells having three or four people looking out to the right to see if there's anybody doing well.

I like to actually have it pretty well-defined who is looking around, a bit like how I described the weather.

If one of my crew gives me a pretty good description on how we're actually going – some days you're going to be going really well and other days you'll struggle for speed – and I'm just trying to see what that is, so for sure I always have somebody.

It generally is the foreward hand, because they have got the best option for vision but it does depend a little bit on the crew and their experience and knowledge.

Q **Brett: You're going out for a training day, what should you practise uphill?**

A Noel: I like defining my practise time pretty clearly on what the goal is for that particular training period.

Essentially, I like to go and say, practise starting and do nothing else but starting.

I prefer to practise trying to hold off somebody just on the hip more so than just straight line sailing to see how fast you are.

Essentially the more difficult things.

Q **Brett: When sailing upwind, what do you look for in jib trim?**

A **Noel:** I'll sail the boat upwind at the angle that I know I need to match the fleet and the jib trimmer will set the jib up how he visually thinks it should look.

All of a sudden you'll find you're well inside of the luff, if that's the angle that we have to sail to match the fleet, so you either straighten the forestay or sheet on, or whatever you need to do to match where you have to sail.

Q **Brett: How important is it to trim the jib in sync with the main? Quite often you see people trim the jib in, and bang, that's it for the rest of the day, they just work with the main, and that doesn't make a lot of sense.**

A **Noel:** It's not ideal that everybody gets labelled as a main sail trimmer or jib trimmer, they should be just both sharing trimming, the overall balanced package.

It's all about balance.

Q **Brett: How important is it to play the jib sheet upwind?**

A **Noel:** I think it's pretty important to play the jib sheet upwind.

The Etchells will accelerate way better with the jib eased and you can almost leave the main at times.

Tactically if we are on a lift, we might decide to use the lift and just rather than sail up higher, closer to the wind, we'll essentially ease the sails and move forward a little bit on the ladder rung.

Q **Brett: What do you look for when trimming upwind sails?**

A **Noel:** I'd probably just use the leech ribbons as a bit of a guide in certain conditions to make sure I'm not too over-trimmed.

Look at the leech and the telltales in the middle of the sail to see, camber wise, if they're lifting or they're stuck or flowing, but also the back wind from the jib on the luff of the main.

If most of the back wind is starting down low in the main sail from the jib, the jib cars will be down too low or in too far, for example.

Trying to work towards getting the even back wind across the luff of the main sail, as long as the main sail's not ridiculously full.

There are things that I would talk to the jib trimmer about. "Hey, we've got a lot of back wind up high", a blowback from the headsail, so then those things create the environment for the two of you who are working together on the package, more so than trimming the individual sails.

Q Brett: The leech of the main does a lot of things, but what do you do in different wind and wave conditions? If it's flat seas you have it set one way, in waves, another way?

A Noel: In Melbourne where we sail a lot, you get such extreme conditions from flat water and bumpy water and tack to tack, it's so different. Starboard and port, so in most cases you have quite a different setup, trim-wise.

If I knew that we are going in to the waves we'll set up for more twist and the main will be slightly deeper for power, across the waves, less twist and a little flatter.

Q Brett: If somebody had to concentrate on one thing above all else, what do you think they should concentrate on to try and improve their sailing?

A Noel: Starting.

If you're going to be racing in a fleet, it's getting the start you want so you can do what you want.

That's the thing I've learned over the years and sailing with some the best people that are racing now, simply it's just starting.

Q Brett: Say you've got a bad start, a lot of what I've been hearing from people is to get clear air straight away, so if you've got to tack away, tack away, get clear and try to find a clear lane and get back into it.

A Noel: You've just got to get clear air.

Q Brett: Do you have a plan, "I know I've got a great spot, but if such-and-such happens, then I've got to tack away" as an example?

A Noel: Absolutely. It's usually pretty obvious if it's going to be a good start or not, and you'll know. You've got twenty seconds to go, hang on, this has got a small chance of not working out here, so very quickly, looking at plan B.

When rolling into the start, I always try to have a bit of an idea how many boats – if it's a group or not just above me, so that I know what I have to do to get up... to tack and get a clear lane and it's nearly always that the earlier the better.

Essentially keep it pretty simple and usually be at where I want to start with three minutes to go and sail away from that spot or, depending on the fleet size I have a pre-determined, clear plan on where I'm going to start.

Q Brett: Going upwind, how do you determine current?

A Noel: There is chart plots, there's tide works, there's lots of things you can look up on the internet to get the actual tidal flows.

On a short, one-design race course, I actually keep it pretty simple, and I just have to know in my mind if it's going from right to left or left to right, and the velocity of it.

As much for sailing upwind and downwind obviously, but more for your laylines.

There's more effect on your apparent wind downwind than there is upwind, I think it's really important to know exactly what the current is doing.

As an example, Cowes was a little bit complex because there was a bit of a bank in the middle, and I think you need to know where the banks are.

I actually had a couple of English guys with me who knew it pretty well, but it was the main bank in the Solent and you had to try to get out of the current, you could sail up the edge of it, or across to one side or the other.

I think it's good to get a chart and have a look at the bottom, you see if the depths do change, because it's such an important factor of current. There are distinct times of the day that flow better than others so it's easy to map.

It's not like wind shifts or windspeed which change constantly.

I have sailed in a reasonable amount of current-affected places, and I always have a pretty clear picture in my head that if the wind didn't shift or change velocity, how would the race pan out?

So you just look at the current alone effect.

FROM OTHER SOURCES

Compass – Reading and Who Should Call It

When sailing upwind the helmsman needs to concentrate on steering accurately and will not be able to watch the compass heading consistently.

Obviously in a single-hander he is chief cook and bottle washer but in a two man boat the forward hand will be looking up the course at competitors, wind shifts waves and of course be keeping an eye on the compass.

In a three man boat, the main hand is best placed to watch and report on compass headings and shifts.

Heel

In a dinghy there is rarely a time when keeping the boat flat is not the ideal.

In a keelboat on the other hand there will be an optimum heel angle for the conditions and this is something that two boat testing will determine.

Feel will be an excellent indicator for whether the boat is heeling too far or not enough.

Trim

Fore and aft trim will determine optimum 'velocity made good' (VMG) in different conditions.

When sailing upwind, the crew should sit as close together as possible to concentrate the weight in the right position and not create a seesaw effect caused by having crew weight further apart.

When sailing off the wind in light air, weight should be further forward to lift the broad area off the back of the boat to reduce drag, the boat should also be sailed flat.

The same applies when going upwind in very light conditions with perhaps a very slight heel to leeward to also reduce wetted surface.

On a reach it is essential to move weight fore and aft as dictated by the waves to promote planing and to keep the boat on the waves.

Managing Oscillating Shifts

With an oscillating breeze, find the median wind direction on each tack.

You need to know whether you are sailing above or below your median on each tack, because this is what tell you whether you are lifted or headed.

Once you figure out your median wind direction and headings, don't stop referring to them. If the average wind direction shifts to the left or right as you sail up the beat, be sure to make a mental note of this and adjust your numbers accordingly.

When you are headed you should not tack at least until you reach your median heading – in many cases it is worth sailing a little in to the header after you have reached your mean before tacking and make sure that it is not a pressure header or the wind is about to flick back.

Dirty Air/Wind Shadow

Dirty air extends to leeward of a boat in the direction opposite to her apparent wind. In heavy air it is not as big a problem and the wind shadow effect does not extend nearly as far.

TAKEAWAYS

- Most shifts happen with a velocity drop or increase. Before the start get a 'head to wind' reading and check the heading in gusts and lulls to see if there is a pattern.

- The mainsheet is the key adjustment for balance and trim.

- Clouds are a big part of upwind strategy and you should watch them as they develop throughout the race.

- Nominate a crewman to look up the course for changes in wind pressure and to keep an eye on the fleet I relation to your boat.

- Always sail the long tack first when there is a course bias to give you more options the further you get up the leg.

- Always trim your main and jib in sync with each other.

- The start is the most important thing to practise and get right if you want to improve your sailing results.

- Always have a plan B when you are starting.

- Clear air at the start is paramount to your success.

- Never start a yacht race without first determining the 'mean' wind.

CHAPTER 11

Reaching

CHAPTER 11

Reaching

> *"Up David, down David, up David, down David! Christ, I feel like a coach in a whorehouse!"*
>
> **– Ed Fracker, sailmaker to the stars**

Angle

Practise and two-boat tuning will help you to establish your target angles, know what angles the boat sails fastest both two sail reaching and with a spinnaker.

Generally work low in the puffs, giving you the ability to drive up into the wind to create more power when the wind lightens.

If there is more breeze early in the leg, drive the boat low in the extra pressure so you can come up as the breeze eases to generate more power in the sails and keep your crew on the wire.

Having learnt your boats optimum angle to the wind for fastest speed will determine how far to come away.

Keep in mind how far off the rhumb line course you are sailing when bearing away because you will need to sail a hot angle into the next mark, which is fine if it gets really light.

If there is more breeze late in the leg, any distance you have given away early in the leg may put you well below the mark.

Crew Weight Position

The harder the wind and higher the waves, the further back the crew weight needs to be in the boat, and conversely the lighter the wind the crew will place further forward.

It is important to 'feel' the boat – the weight too far forward will mean that the boat is pushing water out of the way slowing it down and hindering its ability to get on the plane, and too far back will mean you are dragging the transom also meaning that it's taking longer and more effort to get on the plane.

To use the waves effectively, crew weight should be constantly moving fore and aft to firstly catch the waves and then control the boats attitude, in order to promote and continue planing.

Controls

Leech tension has a great bearing on how easy it is to head up or bear away, and in most conditions you sail with more boom vang upwind than down.

When reaching, the use of the vang will control the mainsail leech and assist steering but generally will be on less than the upwind leg.

Unless you are totally overpowered, the Cunningham should be released and outhaul eased in, plus the rig can be stood up a bit if it was raked heavily for the upwind leg.

Depending on wind strength the centreboard may be raked as well, so the boat does not stagger when hit by a puff, and to maintain balance.

With the board up a bit this also allows you to skid sideways in a heavy puff, helping you to keep on the rhumb line whilst maintaining your angle to the wind.

Never cleat your mainsheet, remembering that as you speed up on a wave or a puff the apparent wind is constantly changing and you need to trim to that.

A mistake a lot of sailors make on a reach is to over-trim the main. Ease it out until it just starts to luff along the mast and then just trim in slightly.

A hint here is if the spinnaker is eased, so too should the main be.

Planning for the Reach

Remember to allow for current. Your research before the race should be put to good use when planning your course between the marks.

Whilst still on the beat, consider the wind strength, whether it is building, weakening or in fact shifting, and most importantly the angle to the gybe mark.

Plan your rig setting changes and try to make them at or just before you reach the weather mark if at all possible.

If boats have rounded before you, observe whether they have headed high or low and whether they are having any difficulty on the leg, making the mark.

Have a plan based on your observations when you are heading to the weather mark but the actions of boats that round just before you or just after you may force you to have a plan B.

Locate the gybe mark just before or immediately after rounding the mark as part of your strategy for the leg.

Leaving the Weather Mark

If you didn't get a chance to set your boat up before rounding the mark, do it first before being in a rush to set your kite.

Many times in the frantic effort to out set a competitor, your boat has been unbalanced and the other team have marginally hesitated but have got everything set perfectly, and have started planing earlier and put a number of boat lengths on you, or have attained a position where they control you…

The basic rig set-up doesn't change a lot from the upwind setting. As an example, if it has been heavy air on the upwind leg and you have been sailing with flat sails, they will need to stay flat for a tight reach.

If you plan to sail high on the reach, do it straight away after rounding the mark, firstly to claim your territory, secondly to get in to the passing lane and thirdly to discourage boats behind you to go higher than you.

The time that this changes is if you are going to sail low and you need power, in which case you will need fuller sails.

Strategic Considerations

On a typical reach, the leading boats extend because most of the fleet sails an arc high of the rhumb line.

Where possible, bearing in mind other competitors, sail as close to the rhumb line as you are able, you will stay closer to the leaders and may gain on them by not sailing any extra distance.

High, Low, or at the Mark?

On a reach the rhumb line is the fastest way to the next mark. Obviously other boats will dictate your ability to sail where you want but wherever possible keep this fact in mind.

The key here is to keep your apparent wind in front of the other boats.

The time to sail high on the mark is when you know that the breeze is building, it is heading, the wind is strong, and you should put some in the bank for the puffs so you can bear away or the boats behind are going high and you risk getting rolled.

The time to sail low on a reach is when the breeze is dropping so that you can heat it up later on the leg to maintain VMG, the breeze is lifting, or when there is a gap behind you and the fleet behind is carrying each other off the course.

Second Reach

Many times the wind may have shifted by the time you reach the gybe mark – you need to be constantly reassessing the next leg and developing a strategy based on the boats around and in front of you.

Many places are lost on the second reach if you struggle to get clear air.

When Not to Carry the Kite

If the conditions are marginal and boats in the fleet are struggling, it sometimes pays to leave the kite stowed.

A capsize or getting carried well below the mark is slow, and if you do initially go without the kite, sail a little high and continually reassess after settling down and watching the rest of the fleet.

You can always set a little later and may not have lost much distance if any, and in fact will gain on the boats that have been over-powered or unsettled.

Big Fleet Considerations

When there are a lot of boats on the course, constantly watching where they are going will have a big effect on your planning and strategy.

Where possible keep away from situations that will see you being dictated to by the positions of other boats.

Plan your gybe so as to avoid the crush at the mark and to avoid getting forced wide. If you are forced wide you may be forced to sail part or all of the next leg in the wind shadow of the boats that have rounded close to the mark and in front of you.

Passing on a Reach

If a slow boat is holding you up, try to pass several boat lengths to windward of them.

By the time they realise you are about to pass, it is usually difficult or impossible for them to head up and defend.

Go for the pass in a puff, if you can get planing first it will be easier.

If they head up to defend it will be tough for them to get on a plane.

Dealing with Other Boats

Anticipate and avoid no-win situations, remember that if you start to get luffed off the course by another boat, both of you will be losing out to the other boats that are sailing the fastest possible course to the next mark.

The last thing you want on a reach is to get involved in a luffing match. In many races, the best strategy is simply to 'push' the boats ahead of you fast down the reach by following behind them and not threatening their breeze.

The goal is to get both of you farther ahead of the pack behind, then worry about passing them later in the race or if an opportunity presents itself.

It's not smart to get involved in a luffing match, bear in mind that you are sailing against the fleet not just one boat.

To Douse or Carry at the Gybe Mark

Strategically the decision to drop or carry the kite at the gybe mark can gain or lose you a lot of places.

Of course, a neat clean gybe and clear air on the next leg is the ideal situation but be mindful of many boats rounding in close proximity to each other and the shenanigans that go on vying for clear air.

Assess the situation, and in some instances dropping the spinnaker, slowing down, rounding cleanly and being able to get above the warring boats before resetting can be a good strategy.

Keeping Your Crew on the Wire

On a reaching leg it is much faster to sail high and powered up enough to keep your crew on the wire, making sure that every time you catch a wave or get a puff that you bear away and accelerate back down to the rhumb line.

You will in fact sail a zigzag course but the extra speed ensures that you will get from point A to point B in the quickest time.

Who Moves First?

The crew should be the first to move physically in and out and forward and back, leaving the helmsman to concentrate on steering and balance.

If the helmsman is continually moving he will often lose concentration and thus not be steering the optimum course.

Having said that, the helmsman must still play his part in movement of weight.

Up and Down on the Wire

On a boat with a trapeze, the crew should be continuously lifting themselves up and down on the wire in conjunction with travelling the gunwale to adjust their leverage whilst on a reach.

The wind rarely remains constant due to the increase and decrease in apparent wind caused by the boat accelerating and decelerating in puffs, lulls and waves.

Catching Waves

Catching waves is a joint effort and is a product of steering, sail trim and crew movement.

The helmsman and forward hand will trim in and out in unison plus move their weight continuously to not only promote planing but to keep the boat surfing on waves.

Leeward Mark Rounding's

Plan well out to be clean around the mark and continually watch behind to ensure that a boat does not get an overlap in the last part of the leg.

Once they are inside you, you're not free to tack and may get pushed to the side of the course that is not favoured or you don't want.

When to Drop Prior to the Leeward Mark

When you are approaching the leeward mark, many times it pays to drop the kite early in order to get to the mark fully set up for the beat.

As you approach the leeward mark you should determine the effect that other boats will have on your rounding.

Too many times in larger fleets, by trying to gain a place or two by dropping late, you arrive at the mark too hot and you get caught up in other boats already there, and you end up going around in bad shape, thus enabling those behind to round cleanly and get inside you.

It may even be, though one gate is favoured more than the other, that it is prudent because of traffic to take the less favoured one to avoid the crush and disturbed air.

A little bit of extra distance sailed in clear air may not be as detrimental as sailing in disturbed air with fewer options due to the large number of boats at the favoured mark, not to mention the boats still coming down the reach who will also have an effect.

TAKEAWAYS

- Practise and get to know your boats sweet spot with regards to angle when reaching.

- Generally on a reach the sails should be powered up unless you were overpowered upwind in which case chances are that they will need to stay flat for the reach.

- On a reach, the rhumb line is the fastest course to the next mark

- Avoid luffing matches, the only winners are the other boats in the fleet.

- Constantly whilst on the first reach consider the gybe mark with reference to other boats, it may be faster to drop the kite and initially two sail the next leg.

- The helmsman and crew need to work together to promote and prolong planing both by trimming the sails and moving weight.

- Before the leeward mark constantly you must be reassessing your strategy with regard to which gate to take and when to douse the kite.

CHAPTER 12

Downwind

CHAPTER 12

Downwind

"Grandmother could trim a kite better than that with one hand."

– Dr Carl, J24

"The left looks good here, but the right might be good as well."

– Self-proclaimed Guru

INTERVIEW

In order to get some insights on what it takes to go not only fast downwind but also go the right way, I spoke to highly accomplished dinghy sailor Mike Quirk from Sydney. Mike currently sails a 505 and also a Tasar, every year he competes in Europe and overseas in World Championship regattas.

Q **Brett: A common theme that has been surfacing from each of the interviews I have done with champions is Preparation, Practise and Fitness. Is this something that resonates with you too?**

A **Mike:** I remember Mike Holt telling me at the presentation when he won the 505 worlds in Kiel. He said to me, "I'm not the best sailor in this room, but I've done more sailing than anybody else".

And that's been a consistent message... I don't know how many 505 Worlds I've been to and obviously, I've been to a lot of Tasar worlds since then. But the consistent message I get when I listen to the world champions do their presentation speech, and the message is always the same. The reason they've won is because they just did a lot more sailing and they put the time in.

Now obviously they were talented anyway. But the difference between the year they won compared to... a lot of these guys have been sailing these regattas for a long time, but what made the difference in that year was the determination to put the time in.

Q Brett: I believe you recently observed a training session with a couple of 505 guys in Sydney.

A Mike: Tracks Gordon was the coach and he trains the Olympic Nacra guys plus Opti's. But the thing that he said that I've never heard said before, was that the difference between coaching the Olympians and coaching the normal sailors, is the Olympians are a lot more prepared to spend the time to do the basic things over and over and over again.

Such as sailing a boat flat. They practise for hours and hours and hours to sail the boat flat.

Whereas we're always looking for something a little bit more sexy. It's got to be about sails, or should I put more rake in? Or should I do this? Or should do the other? Whereas they just focus on those fundamental things.

Q Brett: Is what you are saying, that we should concentrate on practising the basic things?

A Mike: We don't really ever have enough time to go sailing. So we need to get the easy wins with our practice and with our learning. We tend to focus on stuff that's way too complicated and we don't focus on the basics.

The thing that's changed my sailing since when I used to finish mid-fleet to being able to win Nationals. It is basically just sailing the boat fast all the time, and keeping it flat, and keeping it in the right power range.

If you practise that, you get so much further up the curve than if you frig around with all the other things, like buying new sails and trying to understand all the complications that, to this day, I still don't understand.

Q Brett: What are the most common tactical mistakes that sailors make on runs?

A Mike: I would have to say that the top mark rounding and the hoisting and that first part of the run is where most of the win or loss is made. While the boats are still close together.

If had to pick one thing that people tend to do wrong, including myself, with the difference maybe that I know I've done it wrong and I've worked very hard to change it, is rush to put the spinnaker up without sailing the boat around the top mark first.

You've got to bear away. You've got to get it on the plane. You've got to get the mainsail set. You've got to get the jib set.

You've got to make sure that when you do go to hoist the spinnaker, the boat is going full-speed because otherwise, everybody around you is, while you haven't even finished bearing away.

The vang's on too tight. The jib isn't set properly. The crew's gone to get the pole to hoist the kite or whatever.

But the boat still hasn't finished bearing away, so now it's on its ear. So the first 30 seconds to a minute, you're sailing your boat at 25% of the speed of the people around you that are just focusing on sailing the boat.

The single biggest problem we have all the time is rushing.

The biggest mistake we make going downwind is we rush the hoists and we screw up the bottom mark rounding. So that's where most of the gains and losses happen.

Once you're on the racetrack, what tactics are there? I suppose the proper answer to the biggest tactical mistake, particularly in 505s, that people make when they're actually on the run is they don't watch the pressure.

If you sail out of the pressure, particularly when these boats are wire-running, you have to keep an eye on the pressure or you'll lose out big time.

Q Brett: When racing upwind, you avoid the corners and laylines in most instances. Does the same thing apply going downwind?

A Mike: The wind is shifting just as much when you go upwind as it is when you are going downwind. Downwind pressure's probably arguably more important than shifts, but you've still got to go where the pressure is. And hitting laylines, it's really hard to pick a layline from a corner downwind.

If you hit a layline and then you have to come into the bottom mark fully pressured, you've just thrown away hundreds of metres on the racetrack, you didn't need to be that hot.

In fact, sometimes you can't even lay the bottom mark. So I would say that not only is it as important, it's probably even more important downwind.

Typically, downwind, fleets go one way or the other. So that might not necessarily be the right way to go, but if you're leading or you're in a position that you're comfortable with... because remember, winning regatta's not about winning races. It's about keeping your averages up.

So if you're in a strong position for whatever your target position is, it may be that the right tactical decision is to gybe away, but you should never gybe away from your competition.

You might make gains by gybing and playing the shifts downwind, but nobody in their right mind would do that because they're sailing away from the opposition.

Q Brett – What tactical factors do you consider on a run and what tactical input do you get from your crew?

A Mike: The two boats I sail are very different in terms of who can contribute to the tactics.

Unless you're horrible at tactics downwind and your crew is much better, the crew should not be doing tactics because they should be focused on that spinnaker the entire time.

That's because they're the engine. They've also got to, in particular, if there's breeze around, they're doing the kinetics. So they have got to watch the waves. They've got to keep the boat flat. Leaning back in the shoulder straps to drive the boat. So they're doing a lot of the work and they can't do that and look around.

The crew can add most value to the VMG of our team getting to the bottom mark by trimming well and using the body weight.

Q Brett – Do you pull your board up on the run?

A Mike: Generally speaking? No, I don't pull my board up going downwind. As a general rule, downwind I use my centreboard to balance the boat, balance the rudder.

If I've got weather helm and the boat's trying to broach on me, I'll pull it up. I've got lee helm I'll pull it down. So I use it as a balancing thing.

Q Brett – What techniques do you use downwind to catch waves?

A Mike: There's a lot of pumping and ooching and goes on with spinnakers and crews that I disagree with.

Generally speaking, when a crew starts getting carried away on the spinnaker sheets and pumping and doing that work, the boat doesn't go any faster.

All that happens is you screw up the trim of the spinnaker and the slot between the spinnaker and the mainsail.

So in 505s particularly, nine times out of ten, you're better off just steering and trimming accurately.

A really big pump on the mainsheet as you bear away onto the waves.

Q Brett – How important is crew placement and movement off the wind?

A Mike: I find that when we're on the trapeze, that as the pressure is increasing and the boat is coming up onto the plane, you come back in the boat as it takes off and starts to plane and get it on the flat bit of the boat.

The moment it starts to slow down you need to move forward again.

You come aft in the increasing breezes, and go forward as the wind's slowing and the boat's coming off the plane.

If you get caught standing in the back of the boat when it drops off the plane the boat just stops.

Q Brett: How do you set yourself up to get past somebody?

A Mike: If they were similar speed, I wouldn't do anything in particular, other than just focus on doing what I do better.

So keeping the boat moving, keeping the boat well-trimmed, getting as low as you can. Just sailing the boat well so that you take distance out of the person in front of you bit by bit. You don't have to win the race on that leg.

I would be trying to get to their stern at a time where I can just get my nose in underneath them a little bit and gybe inside them on a shift or on the next pressure.

If you've got a boat that's slower than you, it's very difficult to go through their lee. So you need to decide whether you would stay with them and wait for the opportunity to gybe inside them and go the other way.

If it's a long way to the layline, and it's very early in the leg and you want to go right, you've just got to sail over top of them.

Q Brett: If you're back in the fleet a bit do you keep a good eye on the compass going downwind?

A Mike: I don't because I can never remember the numbers. But the real reason is because the angles of the boat sailing downwind change as a result of pressure.

I find it very difficult to pick whether I'm in a lift or a knock from the compass.

The world's most accurate compass are the other boats, you can see knocks by how your bearing is relative to the other boats in your fleet.

Q Brett: Does there come a time when you're better off running straight at the mark or as close to the mark as you can?

Mike: The biggest mistake in 505s I see being made consistently going downwind is they come off the wire but don't bear away to be dead square.

You either have to run absolutely dead square and get the mainsail fully out and get fully presented to the breeze and run dead square, at the same time dropping a bit of vang or you have to be hot and on the wire.

If you get in the middle with both people sitting on the side tanks, you're neither, and that's slow.

Q Brett: How do you protect your lead when you're going downwind, especially if it is in lighter conditions where you're maybe sailing more at the mark and not wire reaching?

Mike: The primary thing you do is stay between the rest of the boats and the mark. You've got to watch the puffs and breeze.

As the wind comes and goes and picks up and drops down, the waves of pressure come down the racetrack.

You've got to make sure that you are in front of each one of those lines of breeze. And typically what happens is the people behind you know what they're doing as well.

They typically will gybe on those shifts and on those pressure lines and then you just go with them.

Q Brett: What dictates whether you bear away or gybe set?

Mike: Typically in bigger fleets you always do a normal set, because to gybe back in towards a hundred boats all coming out to round the top mark would be suicide.

As you're coming into the top mark one of the jobs is to discuss whether or not the pressure is better going down the right-hand side of the run or the left-hand side of the run.

Q **Brett: What's the one tip you'd give somebody that was looking to improve? What is the one thing that they really should concentrate on?**

A **Mike:** Keeping the power in the boat at the optimum point. Making sure that you are using the maximum amount of power at all times. So often, the crews have got their shoulders hunched or they're not fully stretched and the boom's not fully in.

I'm sure it's the same in any class. But in 505s, the difference between the guys that are going faster, is because they're sailing through the water faster more often.

They're doing that because they're really focusing on making sure that they've got the accelerator pressed as much as possible, all the time.

It's about communication.

The moment you feel that you have to start hunching your shoulders or bending your knees because you feel as though the boat's running out of power, you tell me.

The crew says "Is that all you've got for me because I'm about to bend my knees and slow this boat down."

And the opposite happens at the moment I feel that I'm going to have to ease the mainsail because the boats going to heel, I'll say to my crew, "Are you giving me everything you've got? Because I'm about to ease this mainsail and slow this boat down". And you have to do that all the time.

TAKEAWAYS

- The major reason that champions win is that they put the time in on the water.

- Olympians and champions are prepared to spend time doing the basic things over and over again.

- Top mark rounding, hoisting and the first part of the run is often where most of the downwind win or loss is made.

- Downwind the crew's job is to concentrate on spinnaker trim and catching waves and tactics should be the helmsman's responsibility.

- The world's most accurate compass off the wind when searching for wind shifts, is other boats.

- To protect your lead downwind, place yourself between the mark and the boats behind.

- Communication between crew and helmsman is essential in keeping the power in the boat at optimum.

CHAPTER 13

Tactics and Strategy

CHAPTER 13

Tactics and Strategy

> How to win a sailboat race
> *"Start first and increase your lead."*
> **–Buddy Melges**

I had the privilege of speaking with highly accomplished sailor Rob Brown about his take on strategy and tactics, excerpts of that conversation are written below.

Q **Brett: With regard to strategy and tactics, what do you and your crew do in terms of on water tactics, what are the roles of the people?**

A **Rob:** If I was steering a boat, I would be principally concentrating on steering the boat as fast as I possibly can and relying on the eyes and ears of my crew to call the tactics or, if there's indecision, to be able to feed information back to me and involve me in the process of making the decision.

If you're going in the wrong direction, that's not really your problem. You rely on your wind callers and your strategists who's giving you feedback, like where you are on the course relative to your opposition.

Q **Brett: Who does what and what are their key activities?**

A **Rob:** It really comes down to the skill set of the personnel you've got on board. In our situation the main sail trimmer is looking in the boat and he's part of the speed team and he's interacting with you to make the boat go fast.

It's a lot easier for the main sheet trimmer to look at and view the compass and he basically calls five up, five down, ten up, ten down.

Then the forward hand would give you the wind calls.

Q **Brett: I've often heard it said that the crew is 75% of where you end up on the day, do you see that?**

A **Rob:** I think where a lot of people come unstuck is where there's indecision. It's better to make a decision than no decision at all.

I think that the important thing is to back the judgment of the people on board and live by it. Don't question it.

Q **Brett: How far from the bottom mark would you start planning your upwind strategy?**

A **Rob:** Theoretically you should be doing it halfway down the run, you should be thinking about what you're going to do upwind. But if there's boats around you, you're fighting for air, and competing for a position to get inside running at a next mark, then it doesn't give you a lot of opportunity to look around.

With a three-man boat, one crewman should be looking behind, and calling the wind pressure downwind. He should be saying that he likes the left-hand side of the course better than the right-hand side or whatever as you're coming down to that bottom mark.

That really places a lot of responsibility on that person to not get involved in the immediate tactics but to get his head out of the boat and think about the bigger picture a minute, two, three minutes ahead.

Q **Brett: Obviously there's going to be some indicators when you're going downwind as to which side of the course the pressures on when you are planning the next leg, if you're back in the fleet a bit you can look at who's already gone around the mark, what's going on with them.**

A **Rob:** Your compass headings as you're coming down on the bottom mark, tell you whether you're in a lift or a knock. I tend to try and get my head out of the boat and look for... I use the term, dominant pressure... where is the dominant pressure on the course.

If it's in sort of fluky light to medium conditions, my general rule is get to the dominant pressure and then work out whether there's a lift or knock when you get there, whether it's upwind or downwind.

Q Brett: So what you're saying is you sail for pressure rather than lifts generally?

A Rob: Well, if there's no other consideration, go for pressure. Pressure is dominant pressure.

Look, there's no point doing lifts and knocks if you're not in the dominant pressure.

If there's a definite wind line or band of breeze, the obvious thing would be to get to that pressure and then play that pressure.

Q Brett: Do you take a huge note of current? How do you work out where it is and what it is?

A Rob: Well I think that comes down to your research before the regatta, and how much information you can get on tidal flow, and coming up with how dominant the current is in your decision making compared to pressure.

Obviously, there's certain tactics of being out in the current for assistance or getting out of it if you're sailing against it, and that, with experience, becomes really an automatic strategy before the race.

I would be researching that, talking to locals and getting as much information as I can on current flow, months before the regatta.

So realistically when you get there, you're not looking at a bit of paper to tell you where to go.

Q Brett: What is the one strategy that a sailor who has always bumped around the middle or the back of the fleet should concentrate on above all else, to improve their race and regatta placings?

A Rob: If you're not 100% sure on your strategy of whether the right or the left is going to pay, I generally look at where the main opposition are setting up on the start line.

If your top three or four competitors are pushing towards the boat end, in the last couple of minutes, you know that they want to start at the right end of the line and probably go right.

You don't want to go out there are just follow people, but if you're not sure, hedge your bets and go with the good guys.

Tide and Current

I spoke with Andrew Palfrey about Tides and Current and this is what he had to say:

Q **Brett: It's obviously important to know what the tide is doing, what observations do you make on the course in assisting you to know where to go?**

A **Andrew:** a. Ideally, you have pre-gamed the strategy based on the tidal strength, the times and the course location

b. It's good to validate all of the above with physically checking the current, either by tossing an object by a fixed mark or with your eye as you pass marks through the race

c. Big picture, I'd make decisions based upon what effect the current might have on a leg, but also factoring in the characteristics of the wind. That is, if there is current, but it the same side-to-side on the race track, I would cancel that out and focus more on the wind.

Or if the current does favour one side, but the wind-shift/velocity is really big, I would prioritise the wind. Likewise, if I can't see any difference in the wind from side to side, or the true wind direction is steady-state, I would put more emphasis on the tide strategy.

d. Laylines play a bigger part in current, as people will make mistakes with this and over-lay (or underlay at the top mark and hit the mark). I'd be conservative on my laylines, and hope to pick up some gains there.

Q Brett: How do you gather local knowledge regarding tides and currents?

A Andrew: a. We are very fortunate these days to have so much info on the internet that is easy to access. There are also books on the tidal flow in places where the tide plays a big factor.

b. But you need to narrow in on the best resources.

c. Talking to locals regarding local effects like shadows and eddies is also key. I'd make sure I do this for bigger events

d. Sometimes the best resource is your own experience, in practice-racing prior to the event and the early races of a regatta. What happened? When did it happen relative to the cycle? Where did it happen? Why did it happen? Which of the resources you looked at prior to racing were the most accurate in retrospect? What can you trust moving forward?"

Q Brett: The depth of the water across the course will affect tidal flows as will the topography of the bottom, do you take this in to account?

A Andrew: Yes, this is fundamental to tidal strategy. Knowing where you are relative to the depth changes is fundamental to sailing the tide well. Also knowing how quickly the depth changes in different areas, as the flow is generally faster in areas of tighter depth gradients.

In learning the Solent (where I now live), it is really interesting watching good local sailors place the boat. I think that is where I have learnt the most."

FROM OTHER SOURCES

Plan for Contingencies

Always be talking in the boat about 'what if's', and look up the course or down depending on which way you are going, to plan what you will do if a certain strategical situation develops. There is no point arriving on port at the zone to find a wall of starboard tack boats blocking your way.

Plan Each Leg

When you have time and other tactical considerations are out of the way, plan the next leg, consider whether you should be going left or right.

If you round a mark without a plan you may sail part or all of the leg the wrong way.

Tactical Principles

- Always sail on the tack or gybe that takes you closest to the mark.
- Always try to sail the long tack first.
- Sail towards the next wind shift.
- Sail toward and in the most pressure.
- Strive to always sail in clear air.
- Tack or gybe a minimum number of times.
- Have a game plan and a goal for each leg of the course.
- Start with clear air but also where you can put your game plan in to action.
- Although you have a game plan, be flexible enough to change it if need be.

Anticipate Your Next Move

Being able to anticipate what might happen up the track and have a plan ensures that when you do meet another boat on the course, you will not make a 50/50 snap decision that could go the wrong way.

Look ahead and continually be thinking about what if's, so it's one crewman's duty to keep their head out of the boat to continually reassess and fine tune your game plan.

Avoid Bad Air at All Cost

Especially in light air, avoid a competitor's wind shadow or the disturbed air from a number of boats up the course. If someone tacks in your breeze you must do something immediately to repair the situation. Put the bow down and drive through their lee or tack.

It is generally worth doing anything you can to re-establish a clear lane of breeze, you may even need to put your game plan on hold for a short period.

Find and Stay in the Best Pressure Downwind

You may have had a feel for which side is favoured when you were going upwind but don't take this for granted. Keep a designated crew's head out of the boat scouring the course ahead and behind for puffs and more pressure.

Remember the pressure you end up with comes from the direction of the apparent wind, keep your eye trained in the direction that you feel the wind on your face.

Sometimes it is hard to see the wind on the water, so continuously use the performance of fellow competitors to reassess the presence of a shift or more wind.

Stay Between the Fleet and the Mark

Downwind, as you are not able to use your wind shadow to control the boats behind, your best defence is to position yourself between the leeward mark and the boats behind.

This protects you against potential losses if the wind shifts plus the boats behind are giving you great information about the wind that is coming to you.

Laylines

It is a given that you should avoid the layline too far out from the weather mark. This is no different downwind and in fact you should avoid laylines and corners all together downwind except when the boat behind gets there first. In this case it's easy to stay between them and the mark.

Left or Right Up the First Beat

Even the best sailors don't always have a strong feeling about which way to go up the first beat. If you are not sure which side is favoured stay near the middle of the fleet but be observant as to which side starts to pay off.

Once it becomes obvious, head that way, you may not beat the guys that got there first but you should still be in good shape at the first mark.

The information that you have gathered going up the first leg will assist you with your plan for the downwind leg to follow.

Technique for Finding the Best Side, Pre-start

One way is to work out the best side of the course is with your tuning partner. While you sail upwind on one side of the course, he sails up the other. After a couple of minutes, tack toward each other.

One boat should gain, after crossing, head toward the opposite side for another couple of minutes. At this point you both tack back and note the difference. In most cases the boat on the same side will have gained.

Greed and Gambling

Cross the pack when you can, this allows you to always be between the bulk of the fleet and the mark, and conversely don't cross behind the pack unless there is a persistent shift coming.

If you are behind, don't think to yourself "we are behind anyway, let's bang the corner" – this rarely pays and is in fact a gamble.

Data Collection

Collection and recording information should not be restricted to pre-race and, in fact, should be collected throughout the race in order to be able to continually adjust the game plan.

Accurate data as the race develops allows you to be flexible.

TAKEAWAYS

- Planning for the next leg should start long before the windward or leeward mark.

- Always sail for pressure unless there are other considerations such as placement of the rest of the fleet or an obvious major wind shift.

- If you are not sure of a strategy, look where the best guys are going and learn from them.

- Have a list of tactical principles and try to remember them and use them in all racing that you do

- Avoid arriving at laylines too far out from the mark.

- Collect and record data throughout the race and be prepared to modify your game plan based on your observations.

CHAPTER 14

Mark Roundings

CHAPTER 14

Mark Roundings

> *"Try that stunt again and you'll have two (expletive deleted) six-metres"*
>
> **– Jim Kilroy to Ted Turner after Turner cut American Eagle (converted 12-metre) inside *Kialoa* at a mark rounding.**

I spoke to Mark Bulka, World Champion, multiple National and State Champion in various classes about mark approaches and mark rounding and an excerpt of that interview is below.

Q **Brett: With regard to approaching the weather mark what sort of things do you consider?**

A **Mark:** Sometimes it's about what not to do. The big one is to "not" get on the starboard layline too early. The later the better. There is a lot of bad air on the Starboard layline unless you are first or close to it. It doesn't matter how much you overlay, someone's always going to come up and overlay a little bit more, or at the very least give you a nasty lee bow.

When approaching the starboard layline early I will nearly always look to tack back onto starboard for a while and hop on the layline as close to the mark as possible. In a big fleet this golden rule can pick you up a lot of boats.

"We may struggle later on getting to the line-up but I guarantee we'll be 50 meters, 100 meters in front of that guy that just went across our stern or went across our bow and went to the layline too early".

I would rather take the risk and try to find a hole in on the port layline than coming on the starboard layline.

Q **Brett: How would you normally approach a weather mark if you find yourself well back in the mob in a big fleet?**

A **Mark:** If you're looking for a big pick up of places, port layline is actually your best chance to pick up a lot of places.

You can pick up 20 boats in a solid Etchells fleet just coming in on the port layline, but as I said you've just got to be prepared to take a big duck at the end if there's no hole.

It's a risk. I think it works 80% of the time but if it's a really bunched up fleet and there's no holes, you've got to be prepared to go back early. Also know your rules and if you foul another boat; take your penalty.

I work pretty hard on starting, boat speed and tactics to avoid being back in the fleet. So if you are ending up there a lot and want to seriously move forward; work out what is putting you there in the first place.

Q **Brett: When you get to the weather mark, there's a hitch mark in nearly all races these days. Do you have a strategy for that part of the course?**

A **Mark:** We must have a conversation about what the wind's done in the last part. We decide whether we want to go left down the run or go right.

If you're high on starboard tack, coming in to the last bit of the mark, then you've obviously got to be thinking about maybe being on port, you've got to put your bow in a position so you can make that gybe.

Alternatively if you are low on starboard tack coming into the mark you may want to keep going on starboard gybe. You've got to put your boat in a position to do this with minimal effect from others around you.

Or you if want to keep going on starboard then you've got a plan to set up, if you go around with John Bertrand and Cameron Miles and those guys you know they're going to put their bow down and go the fastest way down.

Some sailors are not so clever and will drive the fleet higher away from the optimum course. The boats around you and their actions may help you determine the gybe you take

Q Brett: How far before the leeward mark do you start planning? Do you have someone thinking about the upwind while you're going downwind or is that something you do?

A Mark: I'm always chatting. On a one-man boat, it's going through my head all the time but the decision on which mark can quickly change.

That is our sport and the beauty of it. You may come up with a side of the course you want to start the beat with, which mark however with two bottom marks will allow you to sail your plan the quickest and with least interference. You must be flexible however we will always try to take the quickest option.

You've got to be thinking which side of the course was favoured, are all the boats going that way, is there a big bunch all about to go round that starboard mark?

Are we just going to come around right on their stern, and be forced to tack off where we want to go anyway?

Do we go around the port mark and then go up 100 meters and then tack back onto starboard? There's no one rule for every situation.

Q Brett: Would you take a risk if there's an opportunity to stick your bow in between someone on the mark?

A Mark: I'm 100% by the rules. If you can get your bow inside and you've had the overlap, then for sure you've got to put it in there.

No question, I mean what's your alternative? To put it on the outside that's no good.

Q Brett: Even the good guys sometimes get caught back in the fleet, there may be a situation that a leeward gate mark is further away, it's not the side of the course you want to go to, but the penalty for you speed wise is going to be less than getting caught in a tangle of boats.

A Mark: Every situation is different. Clean air is very important. To be good you've got to be able to weigh up the odds and choose given all the factors. You've got to be flexible.

Q Brett: How do you approach a wing mark?

A Mark: Well, the angle of the reach is really important on the Contender, we still do a lot of reaching, we still do two reaches per race, the two things that are important is that if it's a tight reach, there's no good going low.

If it's a broad reach, you can go low and make up really good ground, and that was really big in the Finns.

With regards to the actual mark rounding itself, it's just the basic stuff really, you just have a nice radius to go around the mark and be able to sail a tight line up if you need to.

Q Brett: Is there any one thing you think someone should do to improve, to get better at this sport?

A Mark: Yes, have the fastest boat and know how to make it go fast.

Do the research and get the best gear. Equally understand how to make it work.

Just get what's going fast, have the fastest hull, the fastest keel, the fastest mast, the fastest sail get all that. Then work out how to make that gear really fast.

What's the spreader angles? What does that need to be? What's the rig tension need to be for what conditions.

Understand what you're trying to achieve. Get past just knowing what the tuning guide says. What are we actually trying to achieve with the rig when we look up?

You can learn so much of this off the water, it might be just picking up the phone, ringing some sailing legend and getting his view, and having a good ol' chit chat and then going to someone else and asking a few questions, just work every element of the boat out.

Don't be happy with anything that's not absolutely perfect, and just keep investigating what it is that makes your boat go quicker.

FROM OTHER SOURCES

Common Mistakes

The most common mistake at a leeward mark is to reach the zone with an outside overlap and then to stay there.

It is better to slow down and round behind, rounding the mark in close, which gives you a chance to sail higher than the boat in front, lock out the boat behind and gives you the option to tack to clear your air if you need to.

Dropping the spinnaker too late and arriving too quickly means that many options for rounding in good shape disappear.

Wide in Tight Out

Always take leeward marks starting wide then finishing tight to protect your upwind lane. If you fail to follow that procedure you will end up in a lower lane than other competitors and start the windward leg at a serious disadvantage.

You may be forced to tack to clear your air and in many cases having to tack away from the favoured side or to have to hold on in order to clear the downwind boats.

Approaching a Weather Mark

Under Rule 18, any boat that tacks in the zone at the weather mark has virtually no rights.

Tactically, it's important to get onto the starboard layline before entering the zone.

If you set up on the layline from a long way out its very risky, you won't be able to take advantage wind shifts, or could have to sail in dirty air if another boat tacks in front of you.

If you are to come in on port, approach the starboard layline at least six boat lengths below the port layline.

Plan the port tack approach as much as 20 boat lengths away but assess what the wind and the fleet is doing.

Approaching a Leeward Gate

Planning for the downwind rounding should start at the beginning of the downwind leg.

You can determine which mark is further upwind generally at the start as long as the gate marks have already been laid.

Be flexible at the gate, when you're in the middle of the pack, you may have to take whatever is available which can mean forgetting the plan you had formed and simply looking for a way to get around the mark quickly and in clear air.

When you approach the leeward gate, one mark is always favoured and generally the best mark is further upwind and is on the side of the course that you want.

Going to that mark allows you to come around in phase or guarantees that you round away from bad air created by the competitors still coming downwind.

As you approach the leeward mark you should have been noting what the wind has been doing during the downwind leg.

Shifts can determine which gate is favoured, and an important point to remember is that any extra distance sailed at the mark is extra distance that you must then sail upwind, thus doubling the disadvantage of choosing the wrong mark.

Tactical decisions should not be ignored though, sometimes sailing a little extra distance will keep you away from the leeward mark crush enabling clear air immediately on rounding or get you to the right side of the course quicker.

Leaving a Leeward Mark

There is an area to windward of the gate marks that is a no-go zone that can be compared to the area below the windward mark.

There is bad air here and very disturbed water, it is often filled with boats going downwind on both tacks meaning your options are limited.

It's not a great idea to round the mark, tack and sail through this zone unless there is a lot of wind in which case the effect is not so bad and tactical reasons may dictate the need to do this.

Rounding to a Run

Prior to rounding the weather mark have a plan for the run, it's way too late to round the weather mark and then work out which way you want to go, gybe set or bear away.

These manoeuvres take time to set up and by the time you are ready the opportunity may have been closed by another boat taking the initiative, you are then dictated to by a fellow competitor and options can be limited.

The Gybe Mark

Wherever possible complete your gybe before your bow gets to the wing mark, this is important so that you can be tight and sail high straight after the mark.

This makes sure that following boats can't get inside you and roll you after the mark on the first part of the next reach.

Strategies at a Mark

It is every sailor's aim to get around every mark as quickly as possible.

Passing as close to the mark as possible ensures that you sail the shortest distance in the race, every bit of distance you lose at a mark rounding is in fact doubled as you now have to sail that bit further.

Obviously other boats at the mark may dictate that you sail around them but be careful not to get involved in their battle.

Big gains can be made by planning a strategy and sticking to it.

To make a split-second change can work if an opportunity suddenly arises, but be careful to weigh up the risks, are the consequences of a collision and is a penalty worth the risk.

Rounding with Other Boats

In a competition you will regularly be rounding with other boats and this can involve a high degree of risk.

The first time around the fleet can get very compressed so it is essential to have a plan and weigh up the risks associated with dealing with other boats.

Think about the consequences of fouling another competitor, the ability to get clear air quickly and being able to go where you want.

Big gains and losses can be made at marks and in many cases losses made at marks can have a disproportionate outcome on your race.

The closer you are to a boat in front the better chance you have of passing it, but beware that that boat may also slow expectantly leaving you nowhere to go except to leeward.

At the mark you must follow a strategy and keep your boat going fast concentrating on boat handling and clear air.

Marks – Tide and Current

An important part of your on water pre-start assessment is knowing what the current is across the course and your investigation prior to leaving the beach will have worked out what the tide is doing at different times during the race.

Knowing the current is essential when planning your approach to a mark and of course making allowances to compensate.

TAKEAWAYS

- Avoid getting to the starboard tack layline too early.
- Start planning your upwind leg while you are still only half way down the run.
- Approach marks where tactically possible, wide in and tight out to protect your lane.
- Get on to starboard before you enter the 'zone' at a weather mark, because any boat that tacks in the zone has virtually no rights.
- Have an accurate picture of current on the course and know tide times – write them on the boat.
- Passing as close to the mark as possible ensures that you sail the shortest distance.
- Gybe prior to getting to the wing mark, this ensures that you can pass close and not allow a competitor to get inside you.
- Every bit of distance you lose at a leeward mark means you have doubled the distance you have to sail upwind to make up for the loss.

CHAPTER 15

Boatspeed and Changing Gears

CHAPTER 15

Boatspeed and Changing Gears

> *"Boat speed makes me a tactical genius"*
> **– Dennis Conner**

I interviewed Mat Belcher, Australia's Olympic medal sensation from the 470 class on the subject of boat speed and changing gears, with excerpts from that conversation copied below.

Q Brett: To check your speed, when is a good time to team up with another boat? Do you have a tuning partner or a training partner that you work with?

A Mat: We try and break it down into a general speed, which we try to do before coming to the events or any of the other training days prior.

Most of our speed work is referenced. An understanding of all the controls and all the tuning of the boat, so we have a really good knowledge of... if we're changing a certain aspect of the tuning, then we know exactly what will happen.

If we're coming out for a race, we don't have a lot of time. Usually, you try to get into the right mindset and it's a bit of a rush.

If we have an opportunity, we'll try and partner with one of our squad members, who we know is good in those conditions, we don't have a set boat, we'll know one guy's really quick in light winds or really quick in strong wind and we'll try and encourage them to do a bit of an upwind.

Most of the time, we'll measure our speed off them. Usually about 30 minutes prior to start, as we get closer to the start, we really focus on the conditions and just get into a racing mindset.

Q **Brett: How much store do you put in the other boat's speed?**

Mat: The one thing about our sport is that it's really hard to be good in all conditions.

You've got your favourite set of conditions that you know you're going to perform well in, and you have a lot of confidence in. Then there are those conditions that you're not good at.

Everyone has their favourite and you need to have a lot of self-analysis, and we say we're not very good in light wind, we need to improve in these conditions, so basically we'll copy them, watch them, do what we can and do as much training in those conditions as we can with them.

And then, whether that's during the event or not, a classic example, during the London Olympics, we were struggling for boat speed with a team that had done a little bit more, they were a little bit heavier, had a little bit different setup.

Even during the actual games we were still, refining our tuning and trying to maximise the speed.

Q **Brett: How important is communication between crew members?**

Mat: I think what's really important is communication in any boat race or really anything, and the communication that Will and I have is extremely important, but it's more the actual type of communication, which is equally important.

Communication with Will and me, because we've done a lot of time together, we have really good synergy together. It's very, very subtle, and sometimes it's not a lot, but it's the right amount of communication for where we're at.

Obviously there's different levels, different forms of communication, for us we just try and be as efficient and as quiet as we can, in that sense that just really creates precise communication between us.

We get out of our rhythm, we get out of our racing mindset if we're talking all the time, it's really hard to actually concentrate and to focus on the individual roles.

Q **Brett: I guess that relationship has developed, as you said, the longer you sail together, the less you need to talk, but you're still communicating, even if you are not talking.**

A **Mat:** I find in a lot of boats, particularly big boats or even in the dinghies, when we talk about communication, a lot of guys just think you've just got to talk about everything.

Every single puff, every single shift, which is really important, but sometimes you've got to balance that with level of concentration, particularly at our level, to really focus on the steering angle, focus on heel, focus on gust response and really just try to maximise speed.

If you're constantly talking, you're constantly getting distracted and that is the same as driving a car or you're doing anything that requires a high level of concentration.

It's very difficult, but you also need to know where to go, so we practise quite a bit, particularly in a high-pressured racing environment, we've got to know what each other's thinking, we've got to be on the same wavelength and have the same belief of where we're going and tuning and all sorts of stuff, so we do that together.

We really try to maximise both of our different skill sets to make the right decisions and also get the best boat speed that we can for the day.

Our talking is quite minimal, some of the basic stuff we won't actually even talk about, we just know what will happen.

Q **Brett: How important are legal kinetics for your boat speed? I actually saw a bit of video of you guys sailing in Rio and Will was really bouncing a lot on the wire, what were you trying to achieve?**

A **Mat:** For the last maybe six or seven years the 470 Class has taken the approach to make the sport a little bit more athletic. In the end it's the athleticism and the dynamics and just being able to physically demonstrate or push your body to produce the speed.

What Will was doing on the wire is very similar to windsurfing, he's fanning the leech of the sail at a higher frequency than the wind... and through normal gusts than if you were very static sailing.

We're trying to create more energy and flow across the sail, so even though it's quite a big sail, with a seven-metre tall mast, there's a lot of power that you need to generate to be able to do it.

He's effectively pumping the boat like a windsurfer and that's been refined over the last four or five years, the majority of the fleets in the world are doing it.

It's very boat-specific, with our class we don't have Rule 42, which is the main limitation in terms of kinetics and pumping in almost every other class.

Above eight knots of breeze, we don't have that rule, so we can do whatever we want to get to the top mark as fast as we can.

We can constantly tack the boat, we can rock the boat and we can do whatever we want above eight knots to make the boat faster.

It's really added a new dynamic to the 470 class and it takes away the responsibility from a judging point.

Q **Brett: How do you trim and sail your boat going upwind, either into or across the waves?**

A **Mat:** It's very boat-specific and I can only really talk from the 470 perspective.

So for me, having someone on the wire, the angle of heel is really critical.

It's making sure how the boat is traveling through the water, through the waves, on top of the waves, and really keeping a constant heel on the boat.

That will change, depending on the sea state. So for me I'm really focusing on stability, just focusing on and maximising the boat's performance through the waves if the boat's really tippy.

Tippy is if you're coming on top of the wave and the boat leans over a lot, and then you're coming in and you fall to windward, then that's really a big signal that something's not right.

Maybe you don't have the right depth, you don't have the right steering angles and you don't have the right coordination with your partner.

For me the biggest indication in waves is having stability, so when a gust comes, you're in control, and it should be quite effortless, if the boat's set up well, you shouldn't have to dump a lot of mainsheet or pull a lot of mainsheet on.

Q Brett: When you're hit by a puff, what do you do and in what order?

A Mat: Basically, if we break it down a little bit, we run off a three-tier set of principles.

The first one is maximising balance. So we have balance, trim and steering, and it's in that order.

The balance, that we're referring to, in any condition is maximising the leverage, so whether that's in any form of sailing boat or ocean racer or whatever, it's just really maximising the amount of power that you can generate.

If a gust is approaching us, then we'll hike first. The first thing we're going to do is try and maximise hike, get out on the wire, in time.

The second thing is trim. So what we're looking at there is if we're... depending on the change in velocity, where the first thing we will do is add vang tension to try and harness the power.

For us, we'll then pull centreboard, then Cunningham, and then maybe jib track back and then, depending on the length of the gusts, if we're completely overpowered, then maybe possibly rig tension, but these are things that we would not necessarily do all at once.

Then if the gust is quite short, we go to the third, and that's steering.

Q Brett: Feel is really important and for someone who hasn't got a great sense of feel, is there something you can do to develop it?

A Mat: For me, feel is just time in the boat.

Most of its relevance for me, is to be able to see the situation. So if I'm looking at the waves, and they're not feeling how it looks or if I'm seeing the gusts, or if I'm looking at the sails and adjusting, it's a very visual type of learning for me and a visual connection.

Both myself and my sailing partner are looking at the same things, and then we can actually discuss, how does that feel? "Does that feel a bit better or worse?"

We're using it as reference to other boats, we're using it in reference to numbers, from a data-analysis point.

I really need to actually look and see, I use everything as an indicator.

Q **Brett: Is sense of feel intuitive or can it be learned?**

A **Mat:** I think it can be learned, 100%.

Q **Brett: When you feel that your boat is slow, what's the first change you can make?**

A **Mat:** I think the most important part is the actual understanding. So if you actually know that the boat's slow, that's kind of a critical step.

A lot of people won't actually break that down, or they'll try and look at different areas, the way a lot people in sport necessarily shouldn't... that old saying, you shouldn't blame your equipment, but sometimes you are actually just slow.

If you need to work on that, you find out who is going fast and look at the differences.

It can be as simple as that, well, if we're not feeling well, then we'll change something, and we'll change something based on our experience that we think would be better.

If it doesn't work, then okay, we'll try something else. And that constant, the constant ability to change.

Q **Brett: What do you do to keep your concentration and to avoid being distracted? Have you got any sort of techniques you use?**

A **Mat:** I've always tried to focus on myself even though we have a partnership, and we prepare individually.

We like to prepare differently, and that's just the experience that we have together and at our level, for us we have a lot of trust between each other, and Will knows exactly what I need to do, and he knows what I need, I know what he needs to do and we do that differently.

If I am not saying much, and he feels based on experience that I should be saying something, then he'll start, slowly to bring in some conversation or he'll bring in some terminology that what we would normally use to help support me.

If I'm needing to concentrate, I'll say, "yep" or "copy that" or... "yeah", I'll just really suddenly try and change the conversation, or simply just say, "hey, mate, I need to concentrate".

What I do sometimes, "We need to focus on speed, let's focus on speed". And that usually means hey, let's not say anything, really maximise and concentrate and talk about speed-specific areas.

So he'll start looking at VMGs, he'll start looking at comparatively, how we're going. Whether the speed is good, whether we're lacking height, then we'll start to adjust the different controls to match, where we are.

Q **Brett: Where would you look to change gears, before or after a puff hits? If you can see a puff coming towards you, do you start to make a few changes before?**

A **Mat:** We do, I guess my experience in this kind of thing is so relevant across classes because we're constantly changing gears, every five seconds we're doing something, whether the gust is approaching, just before the gust, during the gust, after the gust, during the lull.

I think the gusts are very important, but equally as important is the lull.

That's quite critical, that's actually where you lose most of your opportunity to gain is actually during the lull and responding in time to make sure that you're continuing your speed, that you've harnessed all the power, and really trying to get through that lighter period.

Q **Brett: So how do you power up and power down with special reference to the order you do things in?**

A Mat: It's really quite boat-specific... I think you've got the usual basic controls.

You've got your out haul, you'll let your Cunningham off, you'll let all the vang off, and you can put your centre board down, you can put your jib track forward.

There's so many different things, and depending on your boat, if you can control your rake, you can maybe bring your rake up to match.

You can move forward a little bit in the boat, all these sort of things.

You can possibly move your main sheet bridle a little bit more to windward, depending on what type of class you're sailing.

All of this sort of stuff you can do whether the boat's a planing or non-planing boat.

Q **Brett: How important is having systems that work properly and knowing what they do?**

A Mat: A critical part is spending time in the boat, but it's also your understanding.

So typical... for me, is that I sail a lot of different classes, and when we have discussions about what different controls do on the boat, it surprises me that a lot of people just don't know.

They don't know when they pull that rope, what's the effect or what's that going to do?

It's very difficult if you're in a racing environment or you're trying to do it quickly, and the gust is very short, to do all these controls. If you don't know what it's going to do, that's quite a limitation.

You've got to really know and have the feel and play around, and just use all the controls and see what they do, and then you've got a much better ability with your added understanding of them. Practise, keep changing.

Q **Brett: If you were coaching somebody who sails in the middle or to towards the back of the fleet, what is the one thing you would suggest that they need to do to start moving up the leaderboard?**

A **Mat:** Preparation, really focusing on your boat preparation or your crew preparation. The biggest thing for me, is that when you come to an event, everything's already done.

It's the work that... I guess at our level, is done outside of the racing environment. It's preparation, it's the sail testing, it's the time in the gym, it's where you staying in accommodation, it's the training coming into it, the loading of the boat and gear and really looking at the detail.

It's very difficult for people to know that or see that.

It's usually things you can't see that actually make the difference, and for me it's just preparing, preparing well.

As with anything, you do the work beforehand, then the actual event is the time you get to enjoy it.

We're always one of the first ones to arrive and one of the last ones to leave. We've done our research beforehand and we're not coming out there and saying, well okay, there's current, or it's really light wind event, we already have a good understanding of what to expect, and then we could match what we need to compete well.

Maybe that's losing a bit of weight, maybe that's a different type of sail shape, maybe that's a different type of crew selection

All of this stuff is important to performance.

TAKEAWAYS

- Prior to starting a race, partner with someone who you know is fast in the conditions to get your boat set up right.

- Good communication between team members is essential but the type of communication is important, endless chatter is distracting.

- Legal kinetics are paramount to be at the front of the fleet and good physical fitness ensures that you can sail as hard at the end of the race as you did at the start.

- Time in the boat is the best way of developing feel and the visual side is part of feel.

- Adjustments that maintain balance are what you are seeking when you are hit by a gust or sail in to a lull.

- You need to be constantly making changes to your set up with both gusts and lulls getting equal attention.

- You must understand what each control does on your boat and systems must be easy to operate. Regularly practise changing things to understand what each control does so that it becomes second nature.

- Boat and crew preparation are the two areas that you must focus on if you want to improve your sailing results.

CHAPTER 16

Setting Sails, Controls and Effects

CHAPTER 16

Setting Sails, Controls and Effects

> *"The pessimist complains about the wind; the optimist expects it to change; the realist adjusts the sails."*
>
> **– William Arthur Ward**

INTERVIEW

I spoke with highly accomplished dinghy through to maxi sailor and sailmaker Michael Coxon regarding sail trim and unfortunately because of space constraints have only been able to copy excerpts from that information filled discussion.

Q Brett: What's the most important sail control and how does that vary from class to class? I know it's a pretty general question but...

A Michael: The most important sail control for any boat is the sheet tension.

Where the sheet tension will tend to control the twist of the sail and the general drive of it, you can actually then use the subtler controls. Controls include the outhaul, the Cunningham eye.

One very important thing depending on the boat is mast bend and how you achieve the mast bend.

If the mast bend is achieved through having a backstay, it makes the exercise fairly easy.

If it's a non-backstay boat it will depend on things such as boom vang, again, sheet tension; it will depend on if you've got control of the mast at the deck. In other words can you control the prebend in the mast whether through a lever or a chocking system?

Another big variable is rig tension. By increasing rig tension you'll put more compression through your rig and increase, obviously the tension, but also the prebend in the rig.

Q **Brett: How long before the start do you usually set your boat up or do you wait until you get on the course, sail the first leg and see how you are going for speed and height?**

A **Michael:** I always head straight for where the starting boat is because it will put you in the conditions you're going to be sailing in.

A lot of sailing is done in enclosed waters these days. As such you can go from inside bays to out to a little bit more open water, so it's good to actually fast track it to where the race track is and do your pre-race training on the race track.

You'll learn also about the current, the wind shifts. Is it an oscillating breeze or a persistent shift? You'll get a feel for the race track.

Q **Brett: Do you try and sail first leg before the start?**

A **Michael:** I try to. You can never spend too much time. But we're all time-poor these days and with crews and families and so on, so you've got to do the most you can. I think it's about being efficient with the time you have.

What I do say to my guys is when we hit that starter's boat, when we round that starter's boat, let's be ready to race.

That means that you don't get there and find, "Oh, I forgot to put the jib hanks on. I haven't tied the Cunningham eye up". Let's be ready to race and then focus.

Then you switch on and you're actually sailing the first beat effectively.

Q **Brett: Do you do any two-boating prior to the start?**

A **Michael:** I'm lucky enough to do a lot of sailing against and two-boating with people like Tom King.

Use the time wisely to prepare your boat. You could get your gear on. If it's a life-jacket day or you want to put your wet gear on, don't get down there and then suddenly say, "Oh, I'm going to pull my jacket on," and all that because you're just wasting everyone's time. Then you use your time effectively.

Q **Brett: How often during a race do you adjust your settings and what indicators tip you off to make the changes?**

A Michael: Depending on how you're going is how often you're going to adjust it.

If you feel comfortable, you'll tend to not play with things that much. You might make subtle adjustments for conditions. I find that if I feel that I'm off the pace, that's when I'll get more aggressive in what I do.

My golden rule in one design, it doesn't matter who the boat near you is, sail yourself boat relative.

I don't care if that boat is regarded as one of the front markers or one of the back markers. If he's got an edge on you, use your eyes. See where his traveler is. See where his prebend is. How much forestay sag does he have?

The other rule I always have is that most races have two or three beats in them.

So many times I'll come back to the club afterwards, and someone will say, "Ah, I was really slow off the starting line". And I'll go, "Okay, so you were slow off the starting, so how were you up the second beat?" "Oh, really slow still up the second beat." I'll say to them, "Well, what did you change?" "I didn't change anything." I'm back here asking you now. I say, "Well, what you need to do is whether you change something for the better or the worse, if you made a change you would have learned".

Once you are comfortable and well positioned on the run as a team, you need to debrief the beat.

If you do identify you had a problem, for instance you might say, "I think we had a height problem. We were good through the water, but we had a height problem".

If I was on my Etchells, the first thing I'd say, "hey guys, we've got to look at whether we have to control the forestay sag a bit more, so perhaps we should straighten the mast up a little bit with the mast lever and that will instantly give me more forestay tension." We also might want to take the rig tension up a little bit.

While you calmly think about that down the run before you get to the bottom mark and the action starts again, you've made some adjustments. You're ready to round the bottom mark. You're in a new boat and you restart again.

Q **Brett: Could you explain the effects of the major sail shape controls**

A **Michael:** Cunningham on most displacement boats, I don't think is a big deal but you may actually be adversely affecting the sectional shape of the sail bringing the draft too far forward. With modern material and sail design the sail should be built to the intended shape.

Different story if I'm on a high performance skiff like an 18-footer or a multi-hull where the sectional shapes are a lot flatter and by playing Cunningham you'll actually drop the leech out very quickly.

I think the important thing with the controls here are mast bend and how you achieve the mast bend.

It depends on what sort of boat you've got. Whether it be through boom vang load, mainsheet load or the outhaul.

Q **Brett: And any other sail shape controls?**

A **Michael:** And we've been talking about mainsail. When we take headsail, obviously car fore and aft is a big deal with a jib. Again luff tension I don't think is a huge deal with a stable sail. It's mainly car fore and aft.

Some boats have the ability to adjust in and out also, so you can in haul and out haul. That's a big deal, and sheet tension. So with a jib the really critical ones are car position and sheet tension.

Q **Brett: You talked a little earlier about forestay sag.**

A **Michael:** On an Etchells, it's a 40-year-old designed boat with an aluminum rig. It's actually harder to set up than more modern boats that are, say, carbon and so on, because there's a lot more variables, because they get a lot more mast bend.

So you go through a lot more range and to address that the extra mast bend you've got more luff curve. You've got excess cloth in certain conditions. What you do with it, that's the question.

Certainly mast bend and rig tension is a big deal with any set up. General rule is the softer the air, the softer the rig. As the pressure goes up, the tighter the rig. That will then get you a tight forestay and a tighter forestay will give you a finer entry on your jib or a flatter jib.

Just as important to control the forestay up range. It's just as important to have the same emphasis on sagging the forestay downrange because if you're carrying, one jib right through the range from 5 knots to 25 knots, it's only got one shape.

You need to continually adjust the parameters around the sail to actually get the right sail shape. If you've got hollow in the luff of your jib and you're sailing in light air, you've got to reproduce hollow or forestay sag so you don't over flatten the jib.

Q Brett: With a symmetric spinnaker how do you determine 'pole height'?

A Michael: I always put on the mast some reference marks and what that allows me to do is reproduce the butt height of the pole.

The basic rule is for the clews to fly level. That means the sails then in balance. My first goal is to get the clews to fly level.

If you've got your pole too high you'll end up finding that the tack of the sail is higher than the clew. What you'll find out is because it's symmetrical you'll then wash the luff out because it's the top of the pole that effectively flattens the spinnaker. So it will make the spinnaker flatter off the entry and fuller off the exit, which is not normally what you want for an ideal sail shape.

Conditions change on a race track, whether it be the water conditions, number of boats chopping the water up and they chop the wind up, you may find you need a slightly different pole height to account for that. Tune for the day. Learn during the day.

Q **Brett:** It was an interesting comment you made earlier about looking at other boats for a hint of sail trim.

A **Michael:** They've actually got it right and you haven't quite tweaked your settings up, that means open your eyes. Otherwise you find, it's what I call the ping pong ball versus the ping pong bat effect.

In one design, you want to be the ping pong bat. The bat controls their destiny. The ball, the other boats control your destiny.

Its small percentages and being that little bit faster, that little bit higher, makes you the ping pong bat. You control your destiny. You get to take the nice lane in to the top mark rather than that lane's been taken and you're just being knocked around one way or the other.

Q **Brett:** Quite often before the start your pace seems equal with the best, why do the champs continually beat us by so much?

A **Michael:** You're only looking for small margins. It's the subtleties.

The good guys are a little bit more switched on to gear changing. So when they changed gears a little bit quicker than you they gained that two or three seconds.

They look over their shoulder, a shift comes through. You look over your shoulder, I can tack and cross versus I look over my shoulder, I'm locked in. You sail through the shift. They've just been in phase both ways.

If you were five seconds advanced you would have stayed in phase.

Q **Brett:** How do you set your boat up for high mode or footing gear?

A **Michael:** The first thing I do is hike. Get your crew weight out. One thing that costs you nothing is your crew weight. Righting moment, there's no boat in the world that doesn't get faster with more righting moment.

Second thing is, I would pull the traveler up a little further, I will ease the outhaul, and I'll ease a little backstay, all of these things will power your boat up and will give you a higher, slower mode. You only need to hold your lane. Holding lane is a really important thing about one-design sailing.

For footing, I would drop the traveler and ease a bit of jib but its more in the steering, you don't come away many degrees and when you pull away you load the boat and it heels so hike harder, don't lean in to start making adjustments because not only is the weight not on the side of the boat but you have lost concentration.

FROM OTHER SOURCES

Depowering

Feathering or pinching slightly is one method, obviously wave conditions will determine how effective this is because you may need power to deal with waves.

Flattening the sails by bending the rig, pulling on the outhaul to flatten the bottom of the sail.

In a bending rig the mainsail draft moves back and the Cunningham when pulled on moves the draft forward and also frees the leech.

If your boat has a backstay, pulling that on will bend the rig and remove fullness from the main but you need to be mindful of head stay sag when the rig is bent and a mast ram or chocks at deck level will help to control the head stay.

Rake in a dinghy plays an important part in conjunction with raking the centreboard.

Using Telltales

Jib luff telltales tell you if the sail is under-sheeted or you are pinching. In a perfect set up, both weather and leeward telltales are flying horizontally and in heavier air the windward one may be up a few degrees.

It is also important that the series of telltales up the sail break evenly, this will let you know that the car is in the right place as this controls the twist.

Leech telltales on the jib should never stall.

Record Your Settings

A key for success in racing your boat is the ability to replicate fast settings. Small adjustments to sails and rig can make big speed differences.

Make sure that all sheets, control lines, side stays and rig positions are calibrated and marked and recorded so you are able to reproduce fast settings in matching conditions.

Mainsheet

In most conditions a good starting point is to trim the main so that the top batten is parallel to the boom.

Exceptions to this rule are when you are trying to accelerate, develop power by slightly hooking the batten to weather or when you are overpowered in a breeze, the top batten may be angled out by 10 to 20 degrees.

Sheet tension controls twist in the sail which will also have an effect on pointing and heel angle in a displacement boat.

Battens

Battens in a mainsail and jib support the area outside the straight line between clew and head. They tend to be tapered towards the inboard end to help maintain shape.

Different weight battens and different amounts of taper will help determine the shape and depth of the sail and changing battens can mean that a sail can be used in a larger range of conditions.

Outhaul

Controls the shape of the bottom third of the sail and has a lesser effect on the rest of the mainsail. A tight outhaul flattens the mainsail.

Cunningham

Pulling tension on the Cunningham moves the draft forward and also opens the leech and flattens the mainsail.

This control is not as relevant in a displacement boat but is one of the main controls in a dinghy, skiff or catamaran.

Boom Vang

The boom vang upwind actually pushes the mast forward and moves the tip aft, plus flattens the mainsail and also controls the leech twist.

It also has an effect on the jib luff which goes slack as the mast bends so once again mast chocking or a ram is needed to control mast bend.

Vang tension should be roughly proportionate to the wind strength. In light air you will have little or no vang tension through to heavy air when the vang will be on tight and you control power with a combination of sheet and traveller.

Tensioning the Luff

In most boats, both the main and the jib are at their optimum with slight horizontal wrinkles along the luff. If the luff tension is too soft, wrinkles will be too big.

Increasing halyard tension has the same effect as the Cunningham and moves the draft forward.

As the wind increases luff tension needs to be gradually increased to give the optimum shape for the conditions.

Luff tensioning needs to be done in conjunction with rig tension and chocking the mast or use of a mast ram to create the right sail shape for the conditions.

Jib Leads

These should be set so that the luff telltales break evenly up the sail and the jib leech telltale rarely stalls.

The Slot – (Interaction of Sails)

When sailing close hauled, the jib influences, and is influenced by, the mainsail. The jib redirects the wind flow so that mainsail drag is reduced and the mainsail increases the jibs lift, more so than if the jib was set in isolation.

The slot needs to be widened in heavier air to let more air flow through. Jib cars need to be moved outboard and the main needs to be flattened to reduce back winding and drag

Adjusting the Rig for Different Wind Strengths

In lighter air the backstay should be eased off and the rig should be stood up. This reduces prebend and makes the mainsail more powerful.

The forestay tension should be eased which allows it to sag to leeward and puts more fullness into the headsail.

Luff tension of each sail should be eased as well which allows the designed draft position to return to full power which is about 35% fore and aft on the headsail and 40% on the mainsail.

Luff tension can be adjusted by Cunningham or halyard, or a combination of both.

As the wind strength increases it is a case of reversing the above procedure at the same time keeping the boat balanced.

Jib car position, sheet position, outhaul and traveller are also employed so that you end up with the right sail setting for the conditions.

TAKEAWAYS

- The most important sail control on any boat is sheet tension.
- If a boat near you is going better, regardless of whether it is a back-marker or champion, look at what they are doing differently and copy it.
- Cunningham on a displacement boat is not as important as on a multihull or skiff where the sectional shape is flatter.
- As a general rule, the softer the air, the softer the rig.
- Control forestay sag up range with the use of chocks or mast ram to control mast bend.
- To win a yacht race you must perfect gear changes.
- To point higher pull the traveller up, ease the backstay and push the weight out.
- To foot off, drop the traveller, ease the jib and steer away a couple of degrees.

CHAPTER 17

Sails, Hull and Rig Maintenance

CHAPTER 17

Sails, Hull and Rig Maintenance

> *"Prevention is, as in other aspects of seamanship, better than cure."*
>
> **– Sir Robin Knox-Johnston**

SAILS

Lowering and Folding the Sails

As soon as you hit the beach or your marina after a day's racing, drop the sails– you should not leave the sail up flapping about whilst you get changed or chat.

Wash where possible when a sail has had a dose of salt water and dry them, ease batten tension, then roll the sail with the battens parallel to the roll and put them in their sail bags.

If you have to fold the sails make sure that you don't fold along the same fold lines each time.

Spinnakers should be put in their bags dry to avoid colour runs and loosely stuffed in the bag.

Flogging and Flapping

Don't rig your boat then leave the sails flogging prior to going out. The best way to maintain the strength and shape of your sails is to minimise the time that a sail is flapping.

Flogging and leech flutter degrade cloth properties very quickly, and this is especially true with Technora and Kevlar sails.

Reduce Chafe Points on Your Boat

When you tack or are waiting for a start avoid the jib from flapping against the mast where there will be protrusions such as spinnaker pole fittings, mast rams and so on. The more a sail rubs against any part of the boat, rigging or spars, the sooner it is likely to show failure.

Wherever possible use tape or patches to protect that part of the sail that comes in to contact.

Protect From the Sun

Direct sunlight is one of the worst enemies of sails since it will eventually cause breakdown of the cloth.

Your goal should be to keep your sails out of the sun whenever you are not using them.

This is especially relevant at a regatta when the sails may be left in the boat for up to two weeks, so put the cover on at the end of each days sail.

Another good tip is avoid storing them in hot places, such as your cars boot.

Cleaning Sails

Oil, grease, tar, and wax: use warm water, soap and elbow grease. Hard stains can be removed with household bleach or common stain remover. Be careful to thoroughly remove all cleaning solvents or they will damage the finish.

Blood stains: Soak the stained portion for 10–20 minutes in a solution of ten parts water to one part bleach. Scrub and repeat if necessary. Rinse thoroughly.

Rust and metal stains: Scrub with soap and water, then apply acetone, M.E.K. or alcohol. Rinse thoroughly and dry.

Mildew: Hot soapy water is usually all that is needed. If necessary, use the diluted bleach approach. If a residual chlorine smell is still present after rinsing, a one percent solution of sodium thiosulfate will remove all chlorine traces.

Batten Pockets

Regularly check batten pocket ends for wear and get it to your sailmaker as soon as wear is noticed. A sail that has flogged a bit could see the batten eventually flap out should the damage get too great.

Checking Sails and What to Look For

From time to time do a complete inspection of your sails looking for chafe marks, cracks in windows, headboard damage, boltrope wear, batten pocket chafing and small tears that could become big ones if not attended to.

With all sails it's important to inspect stitching, especially in areas of potential chafe such as spreader patches.

On spinnakers, look over the whole sail carefully, since even a small hole could be the start of a large tear.

If you have laminated sails (e.g. Mylar, Technora or Kevlar), check them for areas of delamination. Most sail problems can be patched temporarily with 'rip-stop', but you should have a sailmaker make permanent repairs.

Telltales don't last for ever and these are an important part of sail trim. Make sure you carry spares and replace regularly.

Wind Range

Don't exceed the recommended wind range.

One of the quickest ways to destroy a sail is to use it in more wind than it was built for and in many classes there will be headsails and spinnakers that are cut from lighter cloth for lighter air.

Stay strictly within the maximum wind speed recommended by your sailmaker for each sail. If the limit isn't stamped on the clew, find out what the maximum is from your sailmaker and write it on so your team knows each sail's range.

Check Sail Bags

It is important that sail bags are in good condition and the right size and shape for the sail.

Don't have undersized spinnaker bags in to which the sail must be tightly stuffed.

HULL

Hull Preparation

This very much depends on whether your boat is painted or gel coated.

Gelcoat tends to be high gloss and very smooth so a simple cut and polish with marine grade materials should be sufficient to provide a fast surface.

You should never sand gelcoat without good reason.

If your hull has been painted you may first need to sand with wet and dry paper of varying coarseness finishing with 600 grit paper to get the desired finish.

If there is an orange peel surface you may need to start with anything from 280 to 320 grit.

Cleaning, Sponging

Use a gentle soap with warm water and thoroughly wash with a soft bristle brush then rinse with clean water.

For rust stains, use some Loctite SF 7850 which is a hand cleaner but has pumice in it and will not scratch a high gloss gel coat.

Sponge all water out of the boat when you have finished.

Look at All Sheets and Ropes

All sheets and control lines need to be eyeballed regularly for damage to the outer covering, fraying ends and chafing, then replaced in a timely manner. Do not leave it until it is too late, heavy air has a way of making a small fault a big issue.

Wherever possible leave all ropes and halyards out of the sun, ultra violet light degrades the integrity of the rope.

Shorten all your sheets, halyards and control lines as much as possible. This will reduce weight and minimise the amount of clutter in your boat.

Likewise, control lines and tackles should be checked for chafing and friction in the systems and replaced as soon as wear is detected.

Soft shackles, shackles, pins and points where control lines are tied off need regular inspections to make sure the integrity of the fastenings are maintained.

Often this is where failure occurs and these points tend to be where you can't see them. If need be get a mirror and inspect carefully under centreboard trunks or behind bulkheads.

Trouble Shooting and Maintenance Checks

Check all systems under load for unnecessary friction and wash out and lubricate all ball bearing blocks and traveller cars with a product like McLube OneDrop.

Check sheaves in pulleys for wear, it is common for a pulley which has been grabbing, to have a groove worn in it to the point where it starts to act as a jammer.

Check that all nuts and washers are still tight and have not come loose caused by vibration on road trips or shaking caused in marginal heavy air conditions.

Go right through the boat looking for anything that has become loose and tighten all shackle pins, nuts and bolts.

Buoyancy tanks

Tanks have a habit over time of developing annoying leaks. Boats go through an enormous amount of stresses and strains over the course of a season caused by waves and rig tensioning not to mention crew movement on the deck.

Another thing that causes buoyancy tanks to develop cracks is the pressure build up on a hot day when inspection covers are not removed.

A great way to check for leaks is to cover the tank, its hull joins and fittings with soapy water and then lightly pressurise the tank with air and look for bubbles.

A less sophisticated way is to put water in the tank and look for water escaping. The risk here is that the weight of the water can damage your boat.

Periodically it makes sense to remove all fittings and reseal them. This also gives you an opportunity to check the integrity of bolts that are in contact with carbon fibre.

Inspection hatches are another source of problems and the seals need to be replaced from time to time.

If your deck or side tank is cored, it is essential that when you make holes, seal the fitting and bolt well and if you remove a fitting, fill the hole immediately. If you don't seal against the ingress of water major damage and delamination can occur.

The risks to balsa cores are widely known, rotting from water ingress, and many people think that closed cell foam cores are impervious to water. We assure you that they are not.

While water itself does not directly affect most foams, water does react with the plastic resins and bonding agents used to adhere the foams to the laminate skins.

Once water gets into the core, this chemical reaction then goes to work on the core, softening it to the point where the deck gets spongy and eventually the foam separates from the fiberglass.

Blocks and Fittings

Check all pulleys for load distortion and the same goes for shackles and clevis pins.

Check the spring tension on cam cleats and where possible wash them out and lubricate them, check the teeth for wear and if any sign of rounding exists, replace them.

Look at the teeth in clam cleats as these have a habit of rounding up and eventually do not hold the rope properly. Obviously replace if not up to spec as slippage may only occur in marginal conditions when you need everything going for you.

Sand, Fill and Paint Board and Rudder as Necessary

Regularly remove the centreboard from its case and fill and repair any dings and scratches paying particular attention to the leading and trailing edge.

Most boards are finished with a very high quality two part polyurethane, which forms a very tough, shiny finish.

The blade surface can be improved by careful wet-sanding with 600 grit or smoother sandpaper. This removes the gloss and any orange peel on the finish, resulting in the smoothest, fairest shape possible.

However, wet sanding the foil removes that very tough shiny finish, revealing a softer layer underneath. Once you wet-sand a board or rudder, you will have to keep wet-sanding it, as it will scratch more easily.

A wet-sanded surface also gets dirty more easily, and therefore requires more maintenance than the smooth shiny finish.

Eventually, the foil will have to be refinished, and you can start all over.

Rudder blades must be given the same attention as the centreboard.

An item that is regularly overlooked is the centreboard gasket, check this and if it is distorted I any way replace it. Drag from a damaged gasket is a serious speed impediment.

Check All Bolts Regularly Where They Come Into Contact with Carbon Fibre

Stainless steel bolts that are connected through carbon fibre have a habit of corroding where you can't see, and fail regularly sometimes with only a small rust stain as a hint.

At the end of every season it makes sense to remove all bolts that are in contact with carbon fibre and replace and reseal at any sign of corrosion.

Check Covers for Wear and Tear

Both the under and top covers need to be checked over and any nicks and cuts plus sun degradation repaired.

A small nick or chafing damage can grow very large in a storm or when being towed to the point where I have seen many otherwise serviceable covers destroyed prematurely.

It is a small cost to protect your valuable investment.

Spares and Tools

Periodically go through the tool box and clean and spray tools with WD40 or CRC.

Over the course of a season tools get borrowed and not returned or get used for something they weren't designed for, so look through the box and replace anything that isn't fit for purpose.

Look over your spares box and replenish where necessary.

Plenty of bits will have been used by you or 'loaned' to a fellow competitor so check and buy replacements as required paying special attention to small items such as shackles, rivets, nuts, bolts and washers.

RIG, BOOM AND POLES

Troubleshooting

Rig the boat and work each system to make sure that there is no aspect that is grabbing or has unacceptable friction, and that each system has the correct range of movement that you expect.

Whenever you inspect a fitting, look for obvious problems like rust and distortion and use the magnifying glass to find smaller cracks.

Rust, especially rust that you can feel, and even slight distortions or cracks should be considered serious, and the component replaced

Check all metal and Delrin sheaves to make sure that they are turning freely and have not started to have grooves cut in to them which will eventually lead to excess friction in the halyards.

Check car and track systems for wear and tear, wash dirt out of ball races and spray McLube OneDrop or equivalent in to them. Replace balls which may have flat spots in them.

Knock the bottom plug off and shine a torch inside the mast and boom and look for any obvious sign of wear or corrosion.

Look at every exit sheave and rigging attachment point for signs of cracking and corrosion and attend to them as necessary.

Preparing the Rig for a Regatta

At the end of the season or prior to leaving for a regatta thoroughly inspect your mast, boom and poles for signs of wear that may cause a future failure.

Look for shackles that have distorted or have bent pins, split rings that have elongated or distorted, kinks in rigging wires or broken strands, chaffing in trapeze wires and halyards and corroded bolts and rivets.

Shock cords should be replaced regularly as with constant use eventually they lose elasticity and no longer do the job that they were designed to do.

A thorough look at all aspects of your spars should identify and potential for future failure.

Wash Thoroughly Inside and Out After a Capsize

If you have capsized during a race or regatta it is important to thoroughly wash the inside and outside of your spars.

Remember there are ropes, fittings and shock cords in there that don't operate at optimum if cached in salt.

Check Shrouds and Halyards for Signs of Wear

All halyards need to be inspected where they sit when the sails are at full hoist.

Main, spinnaker and jib halyards regularly have problems where they go over the sheave plus if there is a cleat at the bottom the halyard can become worn or the cleat can fail.

Kinks in shrouds and wear where they go over spreaders require particular attention plus thoroughly inspect roll swage ends where the wire enters the swage for signs of rust and worn or broken strands.

Careful inspection of all terminal fittings is a must. Cracks are usually microscopic when they begin, so use your magnifying glass.

You can sometimes feel a crack with a fingernail that cannot be seen.

Replace anything that is suspect.

TRAILER AND DOLLY

Check Wheel Bearings

Even though most dinghy trailers these days are not put in the water (that is the job of the launching dolly), it still makes sense to check and repack wheel bearings.

Many a regatta has been ruined by a lost wheel which always seems to happen either at night, in a remote location and always on a public holiday or weekend when service is not available.

Check Tyre Pressures

Tyres have a habit of losing air pressure and it only takes a few moments when fuelling up to get pressures right on the trailer and dolly.

Because dollies go in and out of salt water plus are dragged across the sand, the tyres do suffer a lot of failures.

Check Protective Padding

If the padding on your dolly is not kept in great repair, your perfect bottom finish runs the risk of getting scratched and not being as fast as possible.

Check it every time the boat is not on it and replace at the first sign of wear.

Check Lights and Brakes if Fitted

Trailer lights have a habit of failing when it is late and dark. Before setting off on any trip, check brake lights and indicators.

Other drivers need to know what you are doing and a fibreglass boat is no match for 1.5 tonnes of metal.

Trailer brakes (if fitted) should be checked a couple of days before you head off giving you time to remedy any defect and not affect your regatta preparation.

Maintain Registration

Ensure you trailer registration is current before heading off to a regatta. Remember that if there is a problem you may not be covered by insurance if the trailer is not registered.

OVERSEAS TRANSPORT CONSIDERATIONS

Packing for Export/Import

Have plenty of tape, rope, carpet, padding and ratchet straps. You can never have enough and invariably when the regatta is over some may have disappeared during it.

Have your spares, tools, sailing gear in plastic bins and clearly marked with yours or your boat's name and all loose equipment clearly labelled as well.

Make sure that the boat and gear is impeccably clean and have sponges, detergent and buckets to clean your gear after the event so that your boat is immaculate on return.

Customs hates any dirt, sand or seaweed to be attached to your boat or trolley.

TAKEAWAYS

- To prolong their life, don't leave sails flogging and flapping.

- Sails should be washed free from salt, dried, rolled or folded and put in their bags when not in use.

- Leave sails in the sunlight as little time as possible.

- Carbon fibre can cause corrosion to stainless steel bolts.

- Regularly check all nuts and shackle pins to make sure they are not loose.

- Keep all ropes, control lines and halyards out of the sun.

- Wash out ball bearing races in traveller cars, blocks and fittings and treat with a product like McLube OneDrop.

- Trailers are often neglected, but regular checks of wheel bearings and wiring is important to ensure it does not ruin your regatta before it starts.

- Replace distorted shackles, blocks fastenings, sheets control lines and halyards as soon as damage becomes evident.

- Regularly go over your spars for signs of wear and tear such as distortion or cracking and tend to it before it becomes a major problem.

CHAPTER 18

Drills and Training

CHAPTER 18

Drills and Training

"He who loves practice without theory is like the sailor who boards ship without a rudder and compass and never knows where he may cast."

– Leonardo da Vinci

Running races for two hours is not practising.

It's important to have the drills set up and discussed before you leave the beach, importantly with a whiteboard session so each team is prepared once on the water and no time is wasted

There are a set of skills which must be mastered before bringing it all together in a race.

Races should be used as a finale to practice and drills. It is useful to have a short race or two at the end of a training session.

The list below is by no means exhaustive and a coach can add another dimension to your training.

Hold Station Drill – (two boats)

Related to start line, ideal wind condition: 8–12 knots

Must be done in pairs, have each boat set up, about one boat-width away on either side of a mark.

Both boats should try to hold their position next to the mark and keep themselves in line with the other boat.

HOLD POSITION DRILL

Sailors should use all means possible to keep their boats in position including sail trim, weight placement and rudder movement.

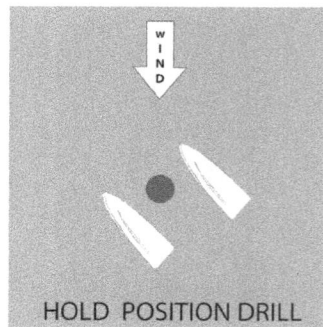

Rudderless Sailing – (one boat)

Improves boat handling, balance, communication and patience. Helmsman and crew must work together through communication to decide whether to use sails or weight to steer the boat.

The most important part is having the centreboard up halfway to balance the boat. It is essential to have the crew work the boat while the skipper focuses on making the boat move fast, it is also important to stress the place patience takes in this process.

Start From Holding Position (Acceleration) – (two boats)

One boat will be holding its position about two boat-lengths from the line.

The other boat will have timed their start and will potentially hit the line at full speed.

The aim of the exercise is to improve time and distance skills and for the stationary boat to develop acceleration skills.

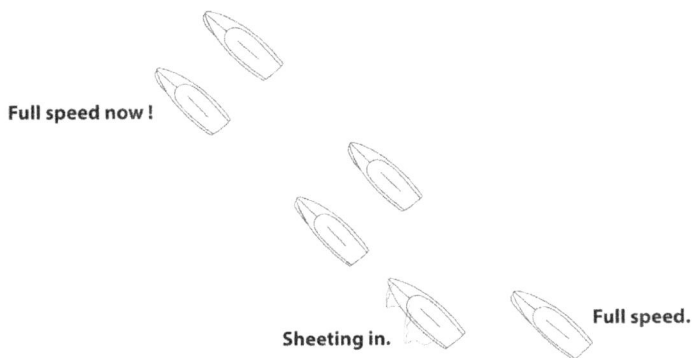

Full speed now !

Sheeting in.

Full speed.

ACCELERATION DRILL

Hold Your Lane – (two boats)

Drills for upwind, especially off the start.

Each boat must hold their lane off the starting line, put in a short windward mark in, a windward mark helps keep everyone motivated to sail fast.

The thing to concentrate on is learning when to foot and when to point.

Other things to practise are setting up on the starting line with a hole to leeward and the importance of getting clear starts.

The key here is a square starting line that is just big enough for all the boats.

This drill works best in medium to heavy breeze.

Reaching – (one boat or more)

Reaching between two marks

On a windy day, set marks about two minutes apart, of course this will be class dependent and extend the distance if you are sailing a 49er, foiling moth or other fast boat, I am sure you get the picture.

The boats must sail between the two marks, working on surfing waves and planing.

The marks need to be far enough away that the sailors have enough time to get surfing.

The things to focus on are body position in stronger winds on reaches, sail trim through waves, ooching and pumping within class rules.

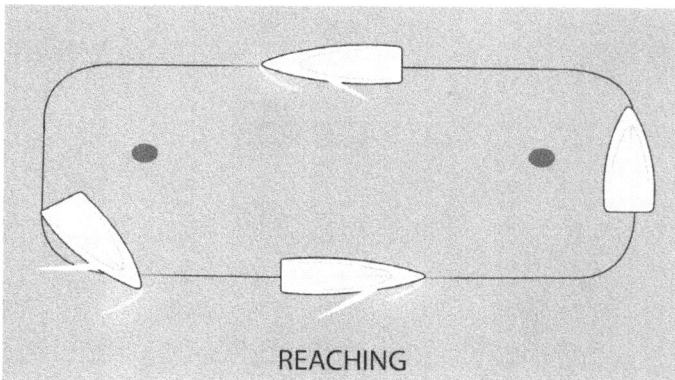

REACHING

Continuous Starts – (two boats or more)

Repetition of starts.

Run a regular three minute start sequence but set your watch so that it continuously counts down five minutes.

After the start sail for 90 seconds and then peel off as you have three minutes to the next start.

Keep sailors engaged in nonstop starting sequences, the purpose being to focus on making quick decisions on the line and getting into place.

Time and Distance – (one boat or more)

Set up two buoys to represent a starting line.

Start on port tack near the place where you want to start and allow three minutes, reach away from the line, then tack and sail back to start.

The goal of this drill is to hit the line with full speed as close to the start time as possible.

Crew Races – (one boat or more)

Helps develop communication between helmsman and crew.

Get the helmsman and crew to switch positions. This will force them to communicate what they know about doing their job in the boat with the other.

To make this drill successful make sure that not only is the skipper telling the crew how to drive the boat, but have the crew tell the skipper how to effectively crew.

Suicide Slalom – (three boats plus)

Plenty of wind is good and a handful of boats is best.

You need four or more marks and they need to be further apart the heavier the wind. The marks need to be set in a row running upwind or offset for tight reaching.

Sailors line up and start at either the top or bottom and through the course.

What you are looking to achieve is the sailors dealing with buoy room, close reaching high/low situations and off the wind boat speed.

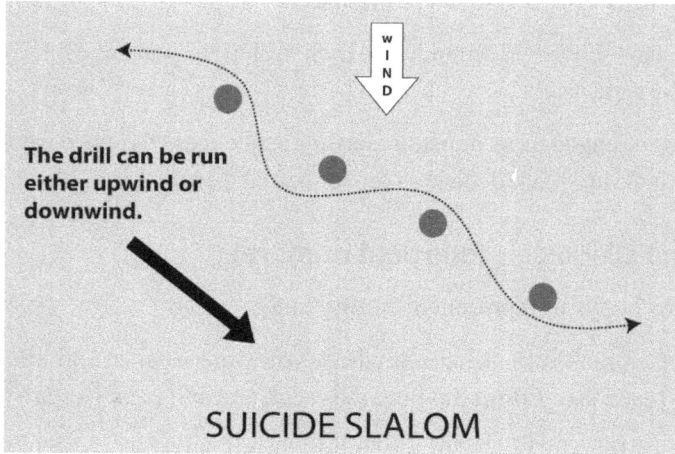

The drill can be run either upwind or downwind.

SUICIDE SLALOM

Upwind Rabbit Racing – (four boats plus)

Particularly good for upwind tuning and speed.

One boat starts on port tack, and the fleet starts by ducking the rabbit and then sailing upwind.

The rabbit clears the last boat and then tacks. The group continues on one tack until one boat is clearly behind.

The slow boat resets the group by tacking and sailing well clear of the fleet and then tacking back.

The fleet then restarts by ducking the slow boat which has now become the new rabbit.

It is important for the new rabbit to set up far enough away so that the closest boat can tack and duck to restart safely.

The fleet will be starting on both port and starboard tacks and will be alternating starting tacks.

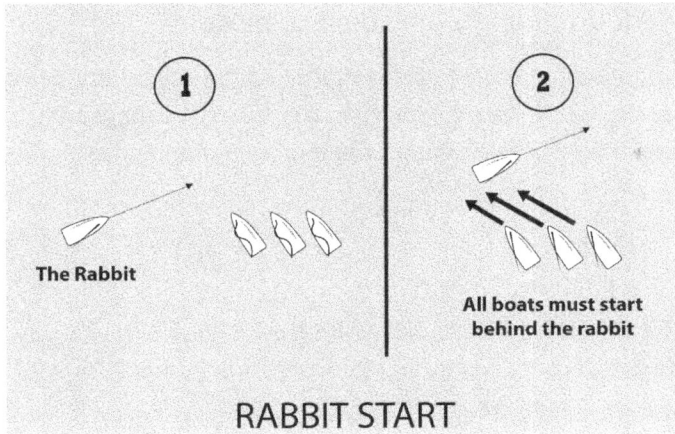

RABBIT START

Downwind Rabbit Racing – (four boats plus)

For tuning while running downwind.

This is a downwind rabbit start, where the rabbit boat has its spinnaker up on one gybe and the starting boats are on the other gybe and have to set their spinnakers once they pass behind the rabbit.

After the rabbit has cleared the starters, it gybes and joins in.

After a period of time a boat that has fallen off the pace makes the call, gybes and resets the rabbit start.

Rabbit Beats – (four boats plus)

Replicating a racing environment with various restrictions.

Set windward and leeward marks with a maximum of 15-minute legs.

Use a rabbit start and race to the weather mark.

The restrictions may be that you must put in six tacks, or you may put limitations on each team with some only able to tack once and others up to four times.

Practise Mark Rounding – (one boat or more)

Find a fixed mark and practise sailing to it downwind paying particular attention to arriving at the mark with spinnaker stowed, settings for the next leg set and approach correctly, that is, not too close or too wide.

Do the same thing but this time going up wind, plan to approach the mark allowing for tide and current and to keep your boat moving fast, making a decision about a gybe set or bear away.

Occasionally call a crash tack as this will often happen in a race situation when another competitor unexpectedly invades your space.

See how far from the mark you have your boat set for the run, you can guarantee that the good guys in your fleet will have travelled less than a couple of boat lengths.

Lee Bow Manoeuvre – (two boats)

Lee bowing means placing yourself to leeward and ahead of a competitor, in this position your boat's wake and sails disturbs the windward boat's sails enough to have it slowly drop back and, if they don't promptly tack away, it will end up straight behind, or even worse for them, to leeward.

To get this manoeuvre right you must practise with another boat, to try to learn this on the race track will ensure it takes you forever to get it right with plenty of protests along the way.

Boat Handling – (one boat)

You can't race effectively if your boat handling is not up to scratch. Practise sailing your boat with a minimum of rudder movement relying on crew weight and balance to assist with turning. Remember that the rudder acts as a brake if overused.

There is no substitute for time on the water so have some practice drills planned before you go out.

Tacking, although one of the simplest manoeuvres, is one thing that a lot crews lose many boat lengths over the course of a race, so don't overlook doing it until it becomes second nature.

Spinnaker sets and drops need to be practised also until you could do them perfectly in your sleep.

Put yourself under pressure – during a practise drop and call an emergency Gybe just as you are about to drop, this is something that often happens in big fleet racing.

As a bonus, boat handling drills can be a good way to develop specific fitness.

Practise Gybing in Big Wind – (one boat)

It is great to practise gybing in all winds but it is heavy air when most problems occur, so don't ignore practicing in big wind and big seas.

To gybe in strong winds, make sure the boat is sailing rapidly such as when surfing down the front of a wave.

As the boat sails away from the true wind, the apparent wind reduces with the speed of the boat, reducing the forces on the sail, making gybing easier.

Make sure the boat is level prior to the gybe because if heeled to leeward, gybing will be harder as the sailboat tries to luff up and turn in the wrong direction.

Once committed to a gybe, don't hesitate, and turn smoothly while being prepared to move fast when the boom comes across.

When the boom swings across the centreline, it is important that the tiller is centred and the helmsman and crew are in the middle.

Practise Laylines – (one boat or more)

Getting the layline right is critical in competitive sailing.

Overshoot and you've wasted precious time, distance and opportunity.

Tack too soon and you'll waste even more time by requiring extra tacks to work further upwind plus the opportunity to get locked out by starboard tackers.

Locate a mark and practise sailing to it, start from about 200 metres directly downwind which should give you time to assess wind shifts, current and enable you to judge distance.

Do it a number of times approaching on port and on starboard.

One Hour Intense Practise – (one boat)

You must always head out for a training session with a set goal in mind, sometimes starting, boat handling, spinnaker work etc. One such multiple-discipline practice session could take the form of the following.

- 20 tacks followed by…

- Five minutes on each tack, trimmed correctly whilst checking compass headings.

- Five bear-away kite sets and five drops whilst completing a port mark rounding.

- Five gybe sets and five gybe drops using a mark to keep you under pressure and to get your timing right.

- 20 consecutive gybes gybing as soon as you settle from the previous one.

- Two penalty turns

- Three practise starts on starboard using a fixed mark

- Practise a port tack approach

The point of this series is to identify a weakness and then work out what you need to spend more time working on.

Capsize Recovery – (one boat)

Practise is essential.

Even the most experienced sailors capsize occasionally and a lot of time can be lost if you are not able to get upright and sailing again quickly.

Unfortunately it is something that most sailors don't practise. When you practise, do it in both light and heavy weather.

The procedure differs whether the kite is up or not. The correct procedure is for a two or more person boat is:

1. Make sure you are both OK.

2. One crew member should release the vang, mainsheet and jib sheet then stow the spinnaker.

3. The other crew member should get straight on the board.

4. If the boat inverts, it is sometimes necessary for both of you to get the process moving prior to one member getting back in the water to be scooped up when the boat comes upright.

5. The crew member in the boat then helps the other member back on board and away you go.

Of course in a single-hander you are on your own (just kidding), none the less practise capsize recovery – the quicker you are upright again, the less distance you lose against the fleet and the less energy you expend leaving you able to compete flat out.

Some Ideas For Developing Your Skills

For many sailors the most rewarding part of yacht racing is learning and improving.

As a bare minimum, you should learn something every time you go out on the water.

1. Try to sail in as many different classes, this enables you to get a fresh perspective on sail trim, boat-handling and tactics.

2. Learn from and imitate the champions, don't be shy to copy the best sailors and keep an eye on the best boats in your fleet.

3. Take the opportunity when it arises to crew for the best guys in your fleet.

4. Most good sailors are happy to share their knowledge and one of the best ways to learn is to discuss what you have learned or what you would like to know with the legends in your class.

5. It's essential to keep a racing diary and some of the things to record are set up that has worked in different conditions, record sail selection and rig tune, wind and current patterns on the course that you sailed on and what you saw that was different on the high achievers boats with regard to set up.

6. Following on from the racing diary, keep a photographic album as well with photos of sail trim, boat layouts plus save video of sailing techniques from wherever you can find them.

7. You can gain a lot by watching yacht races and if you get the opportunity tag along on a coach boat or even officiate on a start boat or mark laying boat.

8. One of the overarching points that has come out of the interviews I have done is the best sailors never stop learning and continue to be a sponge of information.

TAKEAWAYS

- There is no substitute for time on the water if you want to improve.
- The most rewarding practise sessions are those that are planned on the beach with a particular goal in mind.
- Training sessions don't need to be long but need to have a purpose and end goal.
- Practise should not always be done in conditions that you love, you must get outside your comfort zone.
- Keep a racing diary and record all your fast settings and be prepared to update them as you refine your boat speed.
- Not all training needs to be on the water, a lot can be learned from watching videos, webinars and of course reading books.
- Don't be shy to speak with the movers and shakers in your class or the sport in general, you will be surprised with how happy they are to pass on their knowledge.
- Sail in a number of other classes or with different people to learn more.

About the Author

Brett is an author, entrepreneur, real estate agent, business broker and yachtsman.

After leaving school he travelled to Western Australia where he worked in the oil and gas industry prior to setting up a communication business working mainly with the oil and mineral exploration sector.

He started his real estate career as a broker selling caravan parks for several companies. Soon, he started his own business to source and supply cabins to the caravan park industry.

Brett then increased his focus on real estate after earning his Advanced Certificate of Real Estate and his real estate license. One of his first ventures was starting a business that specialised in the sale of caravan parks and motels. He then started an internet-based business that enabled individuals and companies to buy and sell businesses whilst at the same time re-establishing a brokerage business.

Later, Brett purchased the Australian and New Zealand franchise rights for Sunbelt Business Brokers, the largest business broker network in the world. He opened offices in Victoria, New South Wales, South Australia, Northern Territory, and Queensland before selling the master franchise five years later.

One of Brett's most recent ventures is Australian Business Sales. This company specialises in the sale of accommodation businesses.

Brett's professional and social associations include the International Business Brokers Association, the Australian Institute of Business Brokers, the Business Brokers Network of Australia, the International 505 Association, the International Etchells Association, the RS 100 Association, the Royal Brighton Yacht Club, and the Queenscliff Cruising Yacht Club.

Brett is a competitive yachtsman who has competed in many races and championships around the world, he still owns several boats and continues to sail competitively.

He has travelled and worked throughout England, Ireland, Scotland, Wales, France, Denmark, Sweden, Norway, Germany, the United States of America, Canada, Croatia, Hungary, Fiji, Nouméa, Belgium, Lichtenstein, Austria, Greece, Turkey, the Netherlands, Montenegro, South Africa, Namibia, Zambia, Puerto Rico, St. Martin, St. Maarten, Nevis and St. Kitts, Antigua, Mexico, Vatican City, Italy, Serbia, Bosnia and Herzegovina, Czech Republic, Luxemburg, Andorra, Switzerland, New Zealand, Samoa, American Samoa, Thailand, Hong Kong, Singapore, Monaco, St. Barts, Zimbabwe, and Botswana, Spain, Portugal and Gibraltar.

Brett Bowden is the author of *Sailing to Win* and lives in Victoria, Australia.

Brett Bowden Sailing Summary

Country:	Australia
Club:	Royal Brighton YC, Queenscliff Cruising YC
When you started sailing:	Aged 12
Class started sailing in?	12' Cadet Dinghy
Classes you have sailed?	12' Cadet, Soling, Etchells, Int. 505, Flying Dutchman, S 80, Maricat, RS 100
Currently sailing:	505, Etchells, RS 100

MAJOR SAILING EVENTS

Dinghy World championships

- 505 Kiel Germany 1984
- 505 Aarhus Denmark 2010
- 505 Hamilton Island AUS 2011
- 505 La Rochelle France 2012
- 505 Bridgetown Barbados 2013
- RS 100 Bellano, Lake Como, Italy

- 505 Kiel Germany 2014
- RS 100 Riva, Lake Garda, Italy
- 505 Port Elizabeth South Africa 2015
- 505 Weymouth UK 2016

Ocean Racing

- Melbourne to Hobart: four (two as owner skipper, two as crew)
- Sydney to Hobart: five (four as owner skipper, one as alternate helmsman and crew)
- 1980 Cowes Week and Fastnet race: one as crew and co-helmsman – Holland 46 *Marionette of Wight*.
- Devonport Race: two (Crew and co-helmsman)
- Double-handed: one Melbourne to Devonport, one Portsea to Apollo Bay to Westernport.
- Numerous other East and West Coast ocean races such as Perth to Geraldton, Perth to Bunbury, Melbourne to Portland, Melbourne to Port Fairy etc.

Yacht Charter as charterer-skipper:

- Whitsundays x 1
- Greece-Turkey x 4
- Noumea x 2
- Newport Rhode Island USA x 1
- Gippsland lakes x 1

Delivery:

- Melbourne to Sydney x 2
- Perth to Sydney x 1
- Hobart to Melbourne x 6
- Brisbane to Sydney x 1
- Adelaide to Melbourne x 1
- Sydney to Gold Coast x 1

Plus:

- Melbourne to Port Fairy (heaps)
- Melbourne to Portland (heaps)
- Melbourne to Apollo Bay (heaps) etc., etc., etc.
- Fremantle to Geraldton x 3
- Fremantle to Bunbury return x 2

RESOURCES

Join Our Exclusive Membership Site and Enjoy Huge Rewards ....

Twice a month receive lessons via email in the form of interviews with sailing legends, world champions and Olympians.

Receive practical demonstrations, webinars and how to sessions.

All lessons are downloadable so you can revisit them again and again.

Throughout the year there will be BONUS Sessions and offers strictly available to members only.

Inaugural lifetime membership available.

SAILING TO WIN

For more information, contact our office:

📞 +61 417 005 755

www.SailingToWin.com

Proven Formula to IMPROVE Performance and INCREASE Mental and Physical Energy

Sailing requires maximum mental and physical focus over a sustained length of time plus racing sailors also need to perform sudden explosive movements at unpredictable periods throughout a race.

Sailing is not only a very technical pursuit but also requires a powerful body core and draws heavily on the competitor's cardiovascular system.

Sailing races often involve long days on the water and can be affected by unpredictable weather which can extend the time out on the course.

Nutrition and Hydration are extremely important to make sure that you are sailing as hard at the finish as you did at the starting signal.

Peak Performance Supplement and Hydration Collection

Specifically designed for sailors by sailors

- Improved endurance
- Improved focus
- Faster decision making
- Increased and sustainable energy
- Improved hydration

THE ULTIMATE WINNING FORMULA FOR SUCCESS

- Nutrition Bars
- Performance and hydration drinks
- Replace essential vitamins and minerals lost during competition

For more information and orders, visit our website:
www.SailingToWin.com

SAILING TO WIN